GAY
PERSPECTIVE

GAY
PERSPECTIVE

Things Our Homosexuality Tells Us
About the Nature of God and the Universe

TOBY JOHNSON

alyson books
los angeles

MANUFACTURED IN THE UNITED STATES OF AMERICA.

THIS TRADE PAPERBACK ORIGINAL IS PUBLISHED BY ALYSON PUBLICATIONS,
P.O. BOX 4371, LOS ANGELES, CALIFORNIA 90078-4371.
DISTRIBUTION IN THE UNITED KINGDOM BY TURNAROUND PUBLISHER SERVICES LTD.,
UNIT 3, OLYMPIA TRADING ESTATE, COBURG ROAD, WOOD GREEN,
LONDON N22 6TZ ENGLAND.

FIRST EDITION: JULY 2003

03 04 05 06 07 **a** 10 9 8 7 6 5 4 3 2 1

ISBN 1-55583-762-X

LIBRARY OF CONGRESS CATALOGING-IN-PUBLICATION DATA

JOHNSON, EDWIN CLARK.
   GAY PERSPECTIVE : THINGS OUR HOMOSEXUALITY TELLS US ABOUT THE NATURE OF
GOD AND THE UNIVERSE / TOBY JOHNSON. — 1ST ED.
   ISBN 1-55583-762-X
   1. HOMOSEXUALITY—RELIGIOUS ASPECTS. I. TITLE.
BL65.H64J63 2003
291.1'7835766—DC21   2003041809

COVER PHOTOGRAPHY FROM PHOTODISC.

Contents

Introduction

The lesbian and gay rights movement is popularly portrayed as an extremist faction of the sexual revolution. It *is* that, of course, but it's also far more than just that. The recognition of homosexuality as a psychological phenomenon, the rise of openly gay cultures, and the emergence of a distinctive gay consciousness in the last 100 years have prompted fresh questions about the purpose of human life. They have also encouraged fresh inquiry into the function of sex in consciousness, the role of authority in society, the meaning of religion and mythology, and even the nature of God.

We have to ask whether an even larger truth about life and God emerges from the personal experience of us homosexuals because of our uniquely gay perspective.

Uniquely Gay Perspective?

Many people, gay and straight, prefer to emphasize how much gay people are like other people. Don't we want to seem as normal and nonthreatening as possible?

Of course, but we're not normal and nonthreatening. Traditional culture heaps opprobrium upon us, especially in the name of religion. That gay people live positive and productive lives, that we are wonderful people and have important contributions to make to the development of human consciousness, shows us very positively abnormal and threatens the assumptions of traditional culture and religion.

As David Nimmons shows with statistics, hard facts, and anecdotal evidence in his remarkable book *The Soul Beneath the Skin* (a great companion to this book), modern gay men have produced one of the most consistently nonviolent associations of males that has ever existed. For all the problems in the gay world, we're remarkably generous, cooperative, supportive, friendly, harmonious, and peaceful. And what problems do exist—and they are legion, especially in the area of sexual relations—they are almost all products of erroneous ideas about what homosexuality is and who gay men are. Nimmons—who created a New York–based movement of gay-friendliness called Manifest Love—argues convincingly that for our own sakes and for the sake of the larger good, we need to proclaim the truth about our common gay virtue because it's helpful to everybody.

Nimmons observes that if some other voluntary organization of males demonstrated the same civic-mindedness and tendency toward compassion that gay men do, those unusual males would be lauded, lionized, and held up as models for coping with modernization. But because the truth about our lives is distorted, misrepresented, and tarred with the brush of gender-role nonconformity and wanton sexuality, our common goodness is seldom recognized as just such a model.

Our liberation from gender roles and our embrace of the inherent goodness of sexuality make us different from other human beings—and worth paying attention to. Besides, somebody needs to identify and prize alternative views of human life and the nature of the universe, because the current views aren't making this world into heaven on earth. Perhaps we have special insights and special contributions that can help. It doesn't make us superior—or straight people inferior—to proclaim our place in the World Soul. And *we* must do this because no one else is going to do it *for* us.

Indeed, advances in biotechnology may soon make it possible for parents to test for and eliminate gay traits in their offspring. Science may make it possible to delete genetic tendencies toward homosexuality either by aborting future gay children or by "correcting" these tendencies through gene manipulation. If it's true—as so many of us know—that being gay is a blessing, a source of creativity, and a contribution to the evolution of humankind, then we need to argue why homosexuality should not be eliminated from the gene pool. We need to understand why our homosexual viewpoint is something to be protected and nurtured. And we need to tell future generations of homosexuals—which there will be in the near term, at least—how to value their experience positively and productively.

Beyond its place in the sexual revolution, the development of lesbian and gay consciousness is also a manifestation of that dramatic change in culture and consciousness loosely (and sometimes ridiculously) referred to as "New Age" or "new paradigm." This change has been wrought by modernization, increasing psychological sophistication, expanding ecological awareness, the liberation of scientific thinking from the constraints of religious dogma, the ongoing expansion of the human population, and the mingling of cultures and religions worldwide.

The misrepresentation of gay consciousness as mere sexual libertinism is reinforced by the peculiar antisexual obsession of American Christianity and by the political strategy of conservatives, who know the sexual behavior of "other people" is a hot-button issue with their constituents and contributors. Ironically, this misrepresentation is also perpetuated by the protests of gay activists and the pro-sex celebrations of gay culture that inadvertently stir up the wrong voters by pressing that same hot button.

The political goal of the gay movement is certainly to stop the victimization of lesbians and gay men with appeals to simple justice, fair play, and compassion. The movement works to address practical problems that homosexuals face in contemporary society, like holding a job, keeping health insurance, living in intimate relationship, merging—or separating—jointly owned property, being there for one another in health and in sickness, and protecting financial legacies. But there are implications more far-reaching than political gains and legal rights.

In some ways, our opponents understand the consequences of our movement better than we do and therefore become adamant in their objections to what seems so obviously right to us. Religion is often the justification for these objections. Religious conservatives understand that the recognition of homosexual rights compromises the ability of the guardians of orthodoxy to make and enforce rules about morality. It also weakens their claim to a divine mandate handed down through ancient scriptures. If they give in to modern arguments about homosexuality, they may have to give in on many more fronts.

The churches have lost a lot in the last few centuries. They've been proved wrong about the structure of the solar system, the shape of the planet, the course of evolution of life on Earth, the origins of disease and mental illness, the existence of witches, and the causes of "supernatural" phenomena. Admitting that the Old Testament condemnations of homosexual activity are just primitive cultural taboos would further erode the churches' power and authority. Acknowledging that the antihomosexual stance that has been a mainstay of morality is inconsistent with the principles of love of neighbor and respect for other human beings would just show how out of step with modern thinking they've become.

The fundamental issue is nothing less than the origin of truth. Does it come from revelations by God in the distant past that were recorded and approved by church officials? Or does it come from the observation of present reality and scientific experimentation? This was the problem Galileo posed when he announced what he'd seen through his telescope. The liberation of gay voices—part of what we might more generally call psychological sophistication—adds personal experience to the modes of knowing. Is the truth about homosexuality to be found in the Bible or the declarations of Vatican officials, or in the personal experience of actual homosexual persons?

Transformation

Within the various religious institutions, attitudes toward homosexuality, same-sex marriage—and also ordination of women, another gender-role issue—have become the dividing line between progressive and traditional churches. Our issues are at the heart of the modernization of religion—sometimes, actually, without having anything to do with most of us as individuals. It's about modernization itself; we're just the symbols.

Today, we can discern a transformation in the very nature of religious truth. Exposure to the varieties of religion around the world—combined with a commitment to the fundamental proposition that all human beings are created equal—forces modern thinkers to abandon the traditional belief that one culture and one religion alone is right and God-ordained. Modernization and globalization compel us to think from broader perspectives. The study of world religions shows that religious doctrines are more like the metaphors of poetry than the laws of physics. Moreover, it's clear those metaphors emerged from cultural conditioning, politics, historical happenstance, and imagination, not from divinely revealed absolute truth.

We are witnesses to the birth of a new religious consciousness. This new consciousness offers enlightenment and meaning to individuals, even as it poses tremendous challenges to institutions. The gay rights movement is part of this transformation—a reason the movement meets with such violent opposition from traditional religious institutions.

Religion is in dire need of transformation. The model of

God and the world we embrace is supposed to give us a sense of meaning and purpose in life and a clear motivation to love one another and to work in harmony. But the world is in chaos, in great part because of religious conflicts. Because traditional religion opposes gay rights and the recognition of gay people's human dignity, modern gay men and lesbians should be especially motivated to bring about this transformation. And 2,000 years later, this transformation is just the next step in the realization of Jesus' wisdom. The cause of suffering—what we need to be saved from—is not humans' failure to obey dualistic rules about cleanliness and taboos about pleasure, but our failure to love and respect one another and one another's differences.

In fact, today, all of us are consciously or unconsciously adjusting our religious and mythological belief systems to fit modern realities. Everybody has a different idea of what God is; in a pluralistic society with freedom of religion, that is OK with most people. Of course, even in the recent past this hodgepodge of opinions about the nature of God would have been considered heretical. But now it is as natural as curry in Des Moines or McDonald's in Delhi.

Gender Roles

Psychological sophistication and social critique reveal how males and females are conditioned—even terrorized— into traditional roles. In the insightful little book *Scared Straight: Why It's So Hard to Accept Gay People and Why It's So Hard to Be Human,* religion scholar Robert Minor explains how men are taught to be leaders, decision makers, competitors, and warriors. Women are taught to be followers, servants, homemakers, and child rearers. Men are taught to dominate women; women are taught to be submissive to men. Men are taught to suppress feelings and to be always in control; women are taught to be victims of their feelings, to be feckless and needy.

Everybody is supposed to see the world divided dualistically: dominant and submissive, male and female, light and dark, right and wrong. These dualisms preserve the status quo, keeping men in charge—especially men who rise to power within institutions that absorb personal responsibility and free them from accountability. Values in politics and economics are enforced through systems of religion and morality that misdirect attention by focusing on controlling sex and pleasure as though these were the real problems.

These models of men's and women's roles don't apply to modern society. Women are now equal citizens, educated and responsible. A woman is no longer the submissive possession of a man who gives her a name and a reason for living. Reproductive medicine, contraception, sex education, and sexual liberation have altered prevailing arguments about morality.

Gay people, in particular, violate rigid gender roles. Gay people flout societal conditioning and put the lie to the old rules. Beyond our iconoclastic sexual behavior and gender identification, we challenge the very basis for belief in dualistic systems.

Ironically, Jesus and the early Christians challenged that dualistic, male-dominant view of the world over 2,000 years ago. Jesus scoffed at the elaborate taboos of the temple, showing how they contributed to the suffering of the poor and supported the excesses of the rich. He dismissed the dualism of clean and unclean—the essence of ancient religion—by teaching that love and respect for human persons were what mattered, not ritual purity and obedience to every detail of the Law.

Today, the gay rights movement resonates with Jesus' imperative to respect individuals, to respond to human needs, and to treat with suspicion those in authority who tell us to just obey the rules.

It shouldn't surprise us that gay people exemplify certain

spiritual and mystical qualities. Modern gay-sensitive research into history and anthropology reveals that the shamans, healers, and miracle workers who helped to create early human religious consciousness were often people who lived outside convention-al gender roles. These healers and spiritual guides in Native American and other shamanic traditions—two-spirit people—practiced cross-dressing and ritual homosexuality. Many of them would likely be called gay if they were alive today.

And throughout the history of Christianity, people we'd now call gay were the priests, monks, and nuns who chose religious life as a meaningful alternative to marriage and family. Some of these were spiritual pioneers who guided the development of religious consciousness to give profound meaning to life beyond humans' mere animal functions; some also introduced a strain of homophobia into church life that still dogs us today to protect their own sexual secrets.

Most of us grew up feeling we didn't fit—that there was something "wrong" with us and that we were different. If we were unlucky, these feelings of exclusion left us with damaged egos and self-fulfilling prophecies of failure and discontent. If we were lucky, we later learned that not fitting in equipped us with self-fulfilling prophecies of specialness and with useful skills and talents, especially sensitivity to other people's feel-ings—if only in the interest of self-protection and secrecy. Our not fitting in enabled us to develop a critical perspective toward the conventions and assumptions other people accept unquestioningly. From that outsider's point of view we can see how the old mores and beliefs limit and diminish an individ-ual's life experience, perpetuate the victimization of women, justify violence against supposed enemies, and maintain tradi-tional power structures.

If we were especially lucky, we might even have escaped the presumption of dualism—which includes both the notion that the world should be full of conflict in a battle between

good and evil *and* the belief that God and the world are forever separate. We might also have discovered the lesson, so
important in a time of population explosion, that you don't
have to have children to live a good, fulfilled life. In fact, you
make an unselfish contribution to the world by not having
children and by living with no vested or self-serving interest
in the future.

The qualities that support our newly developing religious
attitudes are, first, the ability to see from a perspective that
honors the religious traditions as poetical sources of wisdom
without mistaking them for factual descriptions of the external world and making fetishes of details that no longer fit
modern reality. Second, the awareness that the apparent duality of the world is an illusion and that enmity and competition are not inherent. And third, the mystical sense that we
participate in the life of God in the course of our daily activities regardless of whether we have children. As we move
beyond the confines of traditional culture and belief, gay people embody the perspective that *all* modern humans are called
upon to adopt.

Toby Johnson's Message

Gay perspective tells us important things about the nature
of God and the universe. This book is an articulation of some
of them but certainly not an exhaustive list. Right off the top
of your head, you'll probably notice things the author apparently ignored or forgot. And you may find some of the things
he included incomprehensible. You may believe he ignored
the "real problems" of gay life. That's OK. That you think
about these issues too is a demonstration of the basic message. Indeed, the entire discussion is intended as an occasion
to see how all our worldviews are shaped by our sexual orientation and as a reminder of how different we are from other
people. For this is an important step toward finding our place

in the world and understanding how we can contribute to the well-being of everyone.

This book is more about gay men than about lesbians. This is certainly not because women are less important than men. It is because the author is a gay man who doesn't presume to speak for women. He cannot know women's experience—especially women's sexual experience—firsthand. Moreover, feminist and lesbian writers have already elaborated full-blown spiritualities and worldviews based in women's consciousness. While many of the observations that follow are true for women as for men, they demonstrate a gay man's bias because the observer is a gay man. The omission of women's perspectives in this discussion signifies deference to feminist and lesbian thinkers and writers, not dismissal of their ideas and perceptions.

And the discussion is only about one segment of the gay male population. There are many homosexuals who are not part of this segment and wouldn't understand or care about the discussion at all. But the men of this one segment are an important and visible part of gay community and the "agenda" of the gay movement. These men are deeply fascinated and concerned with religious questions and demand religion recognize their issues. The author believes their concerns and goals constitute what will in the long term prove to be the most important result of the gay movement: the transformation of religion. These men would likely agree with the only partly tongue-in-cheek opening sentence of the author's earlier book, *In Search of God in the Sexual Underworld*: "God and sex: Is there anything else worth talking about?"

Necessarily, of course, the gay perspective I describe in the following pages is *my* perspective—that's all Toby Johnson can possibly know. I offer you a glimpse of the world from my perspective not because I'm particularly important but because the insight I want to share with you *is* important.

And it's emerging in the world through the spiritual aware-ness of many of us. I just happen to be the person writing about it in this particular book. I hope you'll recognize these insights not as special thoughts Toby has had but as realiza-tions *you* also have experienced. Maybe you don't explain things to yourself or to others quite the same way. But I hope you see that these are things—however you conceive them—you already know.

The rise of gay spirituality and the complex of ideas that constitute gay consciousness demonstrate a sort of "collective mind." These ideas are not taught or promulgated in any organized way by a guru of gay spirituality. They seem sim-ply to be springing up on their own in the lives of different individuals. To acknowledge just a few: Christian de la Huerta, Mark Thompson, Donald Boisvert, J. Michael Clark, John McNeill, Robert Barzan, Doug Sadownick, Andrew Ramer, Eric Ganther, Bo Young, and the various contributors to *White Crane Journal*. There are many others writing from within the context of Christian church life.

Some of these individuals are friends or acquaintances, but by and large, the spiritual awakening transpires at the level of the isolated individual. Nevertheless, the articula-tions of this wisdom all bear a resemblance. Articles and books like this one say about the same thing, though from different perspectives and with different terminology. The response from the reading public is usually the same: con-gratulations and amazement that the author managed to cap-ture what the reader already knew and believed himself. Perhaps that's because it's coming from something bigger than all of us.

After all, the same message anchors most mystical tradi-tions: the secret of who and what we human beings really are. It's the patently obvious message of all religion, but most people don't understand it. It's the insight Hinduism conveys in the mantra *Tvat tvam asi,* "Thou art that," and Sufism in its rendering of the Islamic credo *La Ilaha El Allah Hu* as "There is no reality but God." Jamaican Rastafarianism conveys it by teaching that the personal name of God is "I," so whenever we use the first-person pronoun we're referring to God by name. Christianity says it in the words of Saint Paul: "I live, no longer I, but Christ who lives in me." According to the maxim of Texas Hill Country gay sage and Science of Mind teacher Walter Starcke, "It's all God." Indeed, twisting Starcke's maxim into the Sufi credo, we discover that the secret message of mystical religion is the paradoxical dictum, "There is no God because it's all God." In these pages I want to show you, my fellow gay human beings in America in the early 21st century, that you can realize this message—everywhere revealed but everywhere misunderstood—directly from your experience of being gay.

This message of who you really are must be delivered to gay people in a way consonant with gay experience, and not just in forms that have been established by heterosexual society to rationalize its own sexual conventions. The divine message that speaks through the voices of the gods must be articulated in gay-sensitive terms.

For things are changing. The voices of the gods have fallen silent. They no longer speak from heaven above—that turned out to be only sky. The gods now speak in our human voices. It is in human consciousness that the divine now manifests itself to itself. And our gay consciousness, we can discover, potentially speaks to us now—and through us, to the whole human race—that secret message that lies at the core of religion.

This book captures ideas that many of us—gay men, lesbians, and new-paradigm thinkers—are cultivating at this time of transformation. I hope to help us recognize our collective enlightenment, to show how our distinctively gay perspective on reality constitutes a spiritual path, to help us forge a common vocabulary, and to get us talking about our gifts and contributions. The world needs our input and guidance.

I'm not trying to create a theory or system but to articulate, as forthrightly as I can, what is already obvious to us as gay. It's a gay thing, after all, to want to be the little boy who shouts the truth that no one else dares admit: The emperor's new clothes are a hoax and don't actually exist! (Though it is also a gay thing to have devised the hoax and tricked the emperor by his own pretensions.) That's what we understand about many of the beliefs "normal people" take for granted. Our ability to disidentify with collective delusion constitutes a true spiritual path, one born of our homosexual experience. Yet nothing about the benefits of a gay spiritual path invalidates or diminishes the nongay path; we're not in competition with them. We just have our own path.

Homosexuality is not automatically a spiritual path to enlightenment (one of the grouses routinely directed against the gay spiritual movement). But if you're homosexual and you want to get enlightened, then your homosexuality must be part of your getting there. Indeed, the very fact that you feel like you want to be on a spiritual path—the fact that you're reading this book—is the sign that you *are* on the path and that your sexuality is part of the journey. What a neat idea!

A Personal Note

By way of offering a little autobiographical sketch, I'd like to start the discussion with some remarks about my intellectual influences, my choice of terminology, and my reason for believing in the power of self-fulfilling prophecy as the mode of our revolution.

As a Catholic youth growing up in the early 1960s, I was deeply affected by the writings of the Catholic intellectual, cultural activist, and Trappist monk, Thomas Merton. Partly because of my fascination with the monasticism Merton romanticized in his autobiographies, I joined the religious order—the Marianists—that ran the Catholic high school I attended in San Antonio, Texas. I joined out of religious zeal and also because, as I understood later, my constitutionally homosexual soul sought an alternative to the "normal" world of heterosexual marriage and family.

I'm glad I left religious life some seven years later. Like Merton, I discovered Buddhism, and with it a modern, more inclusive religious paradigm. But I'm also glad I had the monastic experience. It taught me about the mystical dimensions of life. And it helped shape my later homosexual experience, affirming the primacy of interpersonal relationship and giving me the faith that true love, separate from marriage and family, was possible and attainable. My path through religious life also got me to San Francisco in 1970 and to an identity as a gay hippie, social activist, and gay-identified psychotherapist.

As I've matured I've come to look like Thomas Merton (that is, like the actor Ben Kingsley). Merton died in 1968, while I was still in religious life but by then in another order—the Servites—where I took Peregrine as a ritual monastic name, that of a 14th-century Servite saint, which means *wanderer*.

Merton's own religious peregrinations were described in a book by his longtime friend Edward Rice called *The Man in the Sycamore Tree*. A couple of that book's last sentences (about the passage from political idealism and social activism to enlightened spirituality) succinctly express one of the messages of this present book. They also reveal the origin of one of the old hippie expressions that I continue to use in these pages. Rice described Merton as "an Englishman who became a Communist, then a Catholic, later a Trappist monk, and finally a Buddhist, at which point, his life having been fulfilled, he died." Rice ends the book with this anecdote: "A hippy said to me: 'Did he give off good vibrations?' 'Yes,' I said, 'he did.' "

Thomas Merton gave off vibrations that deeply affected me and many other progressive American Catholics during the 1950s and '60s. His embrace of Buddhist wisdom foreshadowed the kind of inclusive, transcendent spirituality that grounds this book. Thomas Merton wasn't gay, nor was he a normal, reproducing heterosexual. He didn't live out "family values." In a very real way, this book *is* one of Thomas Merton's vibes. (Though I'm sure he'd have been surprised to hear that!)

As a young teenager, while I was reading Thomas Merton and romanticizing monastic life and the mystical path, I was also devouring science fiction novels. I discovered in sci-fi a kind of mythological language for talking about mystical, paranormal phenomena, but framed in the discoveries and possibilities of science and modernity. I was especially taken with the books of Arthur C. Clarke. His stories conveyed the truly mystical and awe-inspiring grandeur of the cosmos science has revealed in the last century.

In his novel *Childhood's End*—still often cited as the best science fiction novel ever written—Clarke offered an explanation for the nexus between religion and science that 40 years later still makes sense.

Clarke's story is replete with the familiar characters of science fiction: scientists, adventurers, quirky researchers, terrorists, utopians, and ultra-advanced aliens. In the context of this otherwise familiar narrative, he proposed the idea that in the same way a chain of seemingly separate islands is really a range of underwater mountains all connected at the sea floor, so all human beings, though seemingly separate, are part of a larger planetary mind. We're all connected through an "unconscious" substrate of mind. The evidence of this substrate is found in psychic, religious, and paranormal events— from telepathy to miracles.

According to Clarke's idea, the normal course of evolution of intelligent species leads to a merging of individuals into a collective mind that transcends matter altogether. In turn, this collective consciousness merges with a universal consciousness he called the "Overmind." *Childhood's End* follows humanity through the mystical transformation prefigured by religion and realized as the evolutionary apotheosis of planet Earth, complete with a sci-fi FX version of the Apocalypse.

What that meant to me was that these fringe phenomena that were so fascinating to me as a teenager then are clues to the nature of mind. The evolution of consciousness proceeds at the level of this common, invisible substrate. Spirituality is an evolutionary process in the development of planetary mystical consciousness; evolution of mind is what religion is really about.

Clarke's novel echoed the ideas about the evolution of consciousness of the mystic paleontologist Pierre Teilhard de Chardin, S.J. The French Jesuit priest, whose books were suppressed by church officials during his lifetime, argued that evolution is now occurring at the level of culture and mind rather than biology. He predicted human beings would evolve to a collective consciousness and ultimately merge into what he called the "Omega Point." Teilhard was Clarke's intellectual and spiritual predecessor, but his ideas only became public several years after *Childhood's End* was published. Clarke and Teilhard came up with this idea independent of one another.

Clarke's Overmind and Teilhard's Omega Point are versions of God, framed not in archaic religious metaphors but in contemporary terms. For us modern thinkers, science, astronomy, high-energy physics, evolution, and space travel are the modes in which God must be described.

Sir Arthur C. Clarke—knighted by the Queen at the same time as gay icon Sir Elton John—is also a gay man (so probably was Teilhard de Chardin). To be sure, Clarke never styled himself a "gay science fiction writer"—in the way I have with my sci-fi novel *Secret Matter,* which, with a bow to Clarke, gave the arrival-of-aliens setup for *Childhood's End* a decidedly gay twist. Nonetheless, he is a wonderful example of the homosexual as prophet and seer. Sir Arthur—who predicted the development of communications satellites and penned the novel *2001: A Space Odyssey,* another story of mystical apotheosis—is probably one of the most recognizable names in modern world culture. His many novels and his TV series about fringe and paranormal phenomena have captured the imagination of the public with his message about that mystical substrate of experience that explains religion in a reverent but appropriately modern and skeptical manner.

Another who captured the imagination of the public with provocative pronouncements about religion and mythology— and with his own good vibes—was Joseph Campbell, the comparative religion scholar, college professor, and lecturer, perhaps best known for coining the phrase *Follow Your Bliss.* I had been assigned his book *The Hero With a Thousand Faces* in college. It was an eye-opener and the start of my conversion to Buddhist thinking. And so in 1971—fresh out of seminary and studying psychology and Eastern religions in San Francisco—when I learned Campbell was giving a seminar in the mountains above Mendocino in Northern California, I knew I wanted to hear him in person.

Then living as a poor hippie flower child, I applied for a work scholarship. I was asked to come up a day early to help clean the rambling old ranch house where the seminar would be held. Campbell also arrived early. Thanks to that work scholarship, I got to know him personally (and would correspond with him for the next decade). I was also invited to join the team that brought him to the West Coast regularly throughout the 1970s. Joseph Campbell became the "wise old man" in my own spiritual journey. I came to think of myself as a sort of apostle to the gay community of his pro-found but slightly—and deliciously—irreverent wisdom about the real meaning of religion.

Joseph Campbell was not gay—in fact, he was happily and romantically married—but he lived like many gay men: devoted to studying and teaching, and free of the responsibil-ities of fathering a family. His wife, Jean Erdman, was a Broadway choreographer and dancer with her own successful career. Joe and Jean never had children. They saw their books, performances, and other creative endeavors as their contributions to humanity: their "spirit-children." Coincidentally, they lived most of their lives in a high-rise apartment building in Greenwich Village overlooking the intersection of Christopher and Gay.

A few years later, back in San Francisco, while I was working as a psychiatric counselor in a gay mental health clinic in the Tenderloin, I met Harvard-trained political sci-ence and sociology scholar (and nickname-sake) Toby Marotta. After Campbell, Marotta—with his irrepressible enthusiasm for gay consciousness as the flower of modern countercultural thought and his own successful demonstra-tion of revolution through consciousness change—has had the greatest influence on my intellectual life. (At one time I mythologized Toby as my guardian angel.)

Together we launched ourselves into literary careers, beginning with the revision of Toby's massive Harvard doc-toral dissertation on the rise of the modern gay and lesbian rights movement. The product of these labors was eventually published as *The Politics of Homosexuality: How Lesbians and Gay Men Have Made Themselves a Political and Social Force in Modern America*. And we worked together in a fed-erally funded study of gay hustlers and teen runaways, which I summarized in *In Search of God in the Sexual Underworld*. I'd been a gay counselor and activist, but from Toby I learned the rich and complicated history of the movement. With him

I began to understand my interest in religion and spirituality in the context of gay liberation.

The Christian fundamentalists and televangelists are right about one thing: The world has gotten out of whack. People are behaving badly, we are destroying the planet, we've lost sight of the meaning of life, and important values have been turned upside down. But they are wrong to argue that homosexuals are responsible for these problems and that their religion is the solution. In fact, the mythological traditions that are supposed to give meaning and direction to life don't, because they don't make sense anymore. Religion *is* the problem. It hasn't kept up with the changes in human nature, wrought by science and civilization.

The Western notion that life is an ordeal you must survive to get into an otherworldly heaven distracts people from finding and giving happiness now. It keeps them from responding intelligently and compassionately to the problems afflicting the Earth. It keeps them from experiencing the "eternal Now," which is really the only time there is, and prevents them from actualizing the self-fulfilling prophecy that this life really is heaven.

The real meaning behind the various afterlife myths is that heaven exists right here and now. In the words of Jesus in the Gnostic Gospel of Thomas: "The Kingdom will not come by expectation. Don't say: 'It is here' or 'It is there.' The Kingdom of heaven is spread across the face of the earth, and men do not see it."

Those words inspired *Gay Spirituality: The Role of Gay Identity in the Transformation of Human Consciousness*. I wrote that book during the summer and fall of 1999, and turned in the manuscript in October. At that time my partner, Kip Dollar, and I ran a small gay bed-and-breakfast outside Denver. We'd fallen into that life through a curious self-fulfilling prophecy.

In 1981, I'd left San Francisco and moved back to my

hometown, San Antonio. Pursuing the activist identity I'd learned from Toby Marotta, I joined the Gay Alliance and soon hung out my shingle as an openly gay psychotherapist. In 1984, Kip and I met and started an ongoing collaboration as community organizers, AIDS activists, gay entrepreneurs, lovers, and champions of long-term relationship. After several years we moved to Austin, and took over operation of the lesbian and gay community bookstore. Together we ran that business for nearly seven years. After selling the store to a Dallas-based gay bookstore chain, we were ready for another form of gay community service business. We decided to follow our bliss by moving to the mountains and trying our hands at being hermits. I'd just taken over the job of editing *White Crane: A Journal of Gay Men's Spirituality.* A semi-hermitic life seemed appropriate—though with the contemporary business model of the gay B&B.

Though I'd only visited Colorado briefly for a gay health conference, we'd become interested in the state because I'd placed one of my novels there, *Getting Life in Perspective.* In the story, set in 1898, the protagonists jump from a freight train leaving Denver as it snakes up through the foothills. They discover a gay utopian colony, based on Edward Carpenter's Millthorpe Farm, in the fictional town of Perspective, Colorado.

While Kip and I looked at locations around the state, a realtor suggested we make a ridiculously low bid on a house just to "get our feet wet" in the real estate process. He'd shown us a beautiful log lodge that would make a wonderful mountain retreat. But it wasn't near the Interstate or the ski resorts, and it was way beyond our budget. Nevertheless, we agreed to his suggestion "just to get our feet wet." Well, the sellers accepted our bid. It seemed like karmic destiny.

The first month we were there we learned that the nearby state highway out of Denver had been the railroad right-of-way in the late 1800s. The property was located almost exactly where the fictional utopian colony would have been. We called the place Peregrine's Perspective to acknowledge the "coincidence." We lived there three years.

Around Thanksgiving, 1999, Kip's mother was hospitalized back in San Antonio. She recovered from her illness, but we realized we were too far from home and made a decision to move back to central Texas. We put the Colorado house on the market January 1, 2000. In a whirlwind trip in March at the time of our 16th anniversary, we found a house suitable for continuing the B&B business in a cute little artist colony/river resort town in the Texas Hill Country. We moved in June, the same month *Gay Spirituality* was released, with its punch line: "The goal of any spirituality is to experience heaven now." After we got settled and began to explore our new home turf, we discovered another "coincidence": The motto of the town we'd moved into was "A little bit of Heaven."

Of course, that's just advertising hype (and the house in paradise had its own supply of problems, demonstrating that even mansions in heaven require regular maintenance and repair). But it was also a perfect fulfillment—and a dramatic reminder—of the wisdom with which I'd concluded that book.

My Opinion

The ideas that follow come out of my personal experience and history, especially what I learned from religious life, Joseph Campbell, and Toby Marotta, and most importantly, from my experience of being gay at this particular moment in human history. They are neat ideas. But they're just my ideas. I hope you'll find them interesting. But you're welcome to take or leave them as you see fit.

There are many other sound arguments that contradict the neat ideas in this book. That's OK. Truth is very big when you look at it from an enlightened perspective.

So you can take or leave the specific points. But the over-all vision is important to get: We queerly created souls—gay men, lesbians, bisexuals, and transsexuals—have important roles to play in the evolution of consciousness and culture. This realization is an important first step toward proclaiming our freedom to be ourselves and toward claiming our civil rights. It's even more important in our efforts to build our sense of self, maintain mental well-being, follow a spiritual (and blissful) path, and fulfill our fundamental human responsibility to save the world.

With the insights available to us from our gay perspective, let us help create the self-fulfilling prophecies that will transform religion and resolve the problems that face modern society. Let us put out good vibrations.

Chapter 1
Gay Perspective

Being gay gives us a perspective on human experience that is different from that of the great majority of people. There must be something special and useful to humanity about this perspective, since a disproportionate number of important artists, poets, religious leaders, and spiritual guides in the past were what today we'd call gay.

Being gay means living outside the mainstream culture. While for many of us this is a source of real suffering and alienation, for others it offers possibilities for liberation, enlightenment, and artistic creativity. Discovering a positive, enlightening vision of homosexuality helps to resolve that suffering and contributes to the overall well-being of the world. Happy, flourishing gay people contribute "good vibes" that improve—even transform—the world around them.

Because the social condemnation of our sexuality is almost always couched in religious terms, our gay perspective necessarily forces us to seek to understand what religion really is. Indeed, gay perspective is itself a religious phenomenon. And because the social, cultural, and political movements that have bequeathed to us a sense of gay identity are based on notions of "revolution through consciousness change," we have an acute sense of the phenomena of transformation and self-fulfilling prophecy that are at the heart of mystical spirituality.

Since the 1950s and '60s, homosexuals have transformed themselves and their lives—and their place in society—by changing how they conceived their sexuality. Instead of thinking of it as illness or sinfulness, we chose to think of it in the way natural for us: as love and as attraction to beauty and joy. This shift in perspective has changed everything. Signified by our embrace and proclamation of the word *gay* as a badge of community pride, this shift in self-perception has transformed deviant sexual orientation from a terrible burden to a gift from God. No longer a passport to hell, our homosexuality is an intimation of heaven. No longer a sin, it is evidence of grace. No longer a misfortune, it is a sign we've drawn a long straw in this lifetime.

We are still coping with the consequences of this shift in the context of our lives. We are still learning how to practice our sexuality compassionately, still dealing with the issues that have followed sexual liberation (most especially, the daunting spread of HIV), and still discovering the implications of the transformation of our collective consciousness.

Outsiders, Gender Blenders, and Non-Dualists

Gay perspective is based on three specific aspects of modern homosexual experience: First, we are outsiders and strangers. This status bequeaths—and sometimes forces on us—an ability to view life from a critical perspective. Even as children most of us felt "different." Sometimes, often maliciously, our peers and classmates called us "queer," because we *were* queer. We understood things differently from the others, especially things like gender-role behavior in play and sports. We were often more artistic or more insightful. Many of us were teacher's pets, not so much because we were competitive and wanted to win but because we were sensitive to feelings and wanted to be loved. We were often precocious. All of us had a secret, though many of us didn't yet know the words for it, and we may have explained it to ourselves using religious or magical metaphors. We learned how to protect the secret and to figure out in whom we could confide and from whom we had to stay distant. We developed a vivid interior life. We learned to think of ourselves as "special," though we were tormented by that specialness as often as we were secretly elated.

Even those of us who have grown up in relatively accepting recent times—knowing what makes us different and knowing there are others like us—still experienced being different from parents and siblings. We still had to accept that we would be different from others' expectations and that we would have to consciously embrace gay identity, despite considerable social pressures not to.

Because we haven't fit into the conventional explanations of what life is about, we've had to figure out bigger and better explanations that *do* include us. So our outsider's perspective often develops into "higher perspective"—that is, into an ability to see the bigger picture and to understand life in a larger context.

Masculine and Feminine

Second, most of us tend to embody *both* masculine and feminine viewpoints and characteristics. Hence we're able to see both sides of issues and to be both strong and sensitive, both creative and receptive. We blend male and female not to confuse sexual identity but to demonstrate what's natural and best in both sides of humanity. We tend to empathize with both men and women. For this reason we are often good marriage counselors and therapists. We're often less inhibited than straight people about gender-specific traits. And sometimes we even naturally flout gender proscriptions. A gay man, for instance, is less likely than a straight man to be embarrassed to hold a woman's purse for her, even when the straight man in question is the woman's husband.

In fact, we gay folks are often fascinated by transgression of gender roles. We might *enjoy* holding the purse just for the style and verve of it. We enjoy cooking and housekeeping *and* cutting the grass and fixing things around the house. We may enjoy dressing flamboyantly or wearing costumes. We can be "creative" about our dress and appearance. Our voices are more modulated, our facial expressions are more animated and demonstrative. Gay men use their hands more in conversation, make larger gestures, and are less constricted by the fear of looking feminine. For the same reason, we're often less likely to suppress feelings and emotional reactions for the sake of a socially approved effort to look manly. Our body movements are often more fluid; unlike most straight men, we love to dance. We're more comfortable in our bodies. We recognize straightness in a man by his stiffness, physical rigidity, lack of expressiveness, and his fear of looking unmanly.

Straight men, after all, have to be constantly vigilant not to compromise their masculinity. One false step and they may look less manly to their peers. They must constantly prove they are real men by showing they're not the least bit womanly or "queer." It's a heavy burden to never let your guard down. Gay men—and enlightened heterosexual men, who are comfortable with their sexuality, as the saying goes—don't have nearly as much to prove, especially to themselves. We've already lost the battle; we don't have to care. We're less likely to worry about looking masculine than about looking sexy. It's less important that other men think we look manly than that they desire us.

This liberation from the duty to prove masculinity makes us less violent, more prone to empathize with others, less guarded, and more conscious of our own feelings. On the other hand, many homosexuals find themselves in just the opposite situation: They must constantly hide their homosexuality and protect their secret for fear of reprisal and prejudice. However, the difference is that gay men know they're hiding to protect themselves. Straight men conceal their feelings automatically or because they think such restraint is mandatory and should be mandatory. Gay men can find a gay bar or take a vacation to San Francisco, breathe "gay air," and leave the worries behind. Straight men carry the worry with them everywhere because it's not just other people they have to convince of their masculinity: They have to convince themselves as well.

There's also an innocence and simplicity to gay consciousness, despite all the pressures to make us feel guilty and ashamed. Our sexual feelings for our own bodies and our sexual feelings for others' bodies are the same. Our feelings of friendship and affection for our peers and playmates just naturally develop into sexual attraction and infatuation as we discover our sexuality. During puberty we don't have to reorient our emotional lives and attractions away from our friends, whom we understand and share so much with, and toward members of the opposite sex, whom we don't understand and with whom we don't share much except heterosexual compatibility. We don't suffer the straight man's conflict between his private, essentially homosexual, excitement with his own body and his public identity as a heterosexual. Men who find other men's bodies repugnant must have conflicting feelings about masturbation and about the male sexuality of their own bodies.

For straight people, gender is about what they are not: the other gender. Masculinity and femininity are defined in terms of difference. Straight men express gender by avoiding the expressions of the opposite gender. Our gay perspective helps us see that the simplistic and monolithic two-gender system doesn't adequately describe actual human experience. All sorts of varieties and variations in gender expression can be found throughout the history of human culture, and modern freedoms allow even more variations to flourish. Premodern and non-Western cultures have configured gender in very different ways. Gender is much more fluid and eclectic than the two-gender system allows.

Bisexuality, transsexuality, transgenderedness, modern queer identity, and premodern two-spirit identity are all different and separate phenomena—as are male homosexuality and female homosexuality, for that matter—with their own distinctive experiences and exigencies. All these variations are subsumed, at least practically, in the word *gay*. They are aspects of our gay gender-transcendent consciousness.

Because gay people can blend gender, you might say we're liberated from gender. We're neither masculine nor feminine; we're just ourselves.

Nonpolarization

Third, by transgressing normal sexual and gender roles and by transcending the polarities of male and female, we see beyond the entire array of polarities humanity projects onto nature. We don't see the world divided between warring or competing factions the way "normal" people generally do. We don't need to prove our masculinity by imposing male domination on the universe. We're more apt to perceive the unity underlying the duality.

There is a real epistemological difference in our view of the world. Recognizing and coming to terms with our homosexuality—which is what "being gay" means—changes the way we experience reality.

In mythic and metaphorical terms, we are more likely to see the universe the way God sees it—freed from the blinders of duality and polarization. The effort to see beyond duality is the aim of most religious and mystical traditions; it is specifically identified as the foundation of the yogic traditions of Hinduism and Buddhism. Most of us gay people, as a side effect of our sexual abnormality, are bestowed by the universe with this gift of insight. The trick for us, of course, is to recognize and embrace the gift.

The duality we *do* experience is right/left, conscious/unconscious, voluntary/autonomic, objective/subjective, I/not I. But always our insight is that the binary opposites are just different sides of the same thing, not conflicting polarities. The inside and outside of a cup are not at odds with one another. The same is true of the categories male and female. But it is very hard for heterosexual people to see male and female as different sides of the same phenomenon because in the experience of most heterosexual people, they just aren't. By definition, heterosexuals are either male or female, never both.

When we rise to a higher perspective we discover these seeming dualities are in fact one phenomenon. This is a mystical realization. It's the revelation of Self itself.

This third aspect of gay consciousness—non-duality—encompasses the first two aspects: outsiderness and genderlessness. Genderlessness is outsiderness is perspective. The essential nature of gay spiritual perspective is nonpolarized.

Double Vision

Another meaning of duality *does* apply to us. This is the "double vision" that poet William Blake wrote about: the ability to see things in more than one way, to entertain both a realistic understanding and a mythological/imaginative/artistic vision of the same event. To use a Blakean image, this means to see the rising sun both as a shiny disk about the size of a coin above the horizon *and* as the ascent of the Heavenly Host singing "Holy, holy, holy." This double vision means not being trapped in literal, single-vision, black-and-white thinking. It's seeing the shades of gray. Double vision is only possible when you don't believe in simple duality—in either/or propositions. It's the opposite of "I'm right and you're wrong." It's the realization that things look different from different perspectives. This duality allows you to think both literally and figuratively at the same time. It frees you from the obsession with being right—one of the sources of ego, regressive self-interest, and strife.

Rather than duality, perhaps this double vision should be called "plurality" (though that word is used usually to mean a candidate in an election who has received the most votes but not a majority of votes). In religion this is called polytheism: the idea that there are many gods and that belief in one God doesn't conflict with others' beliefs in other gods. (Judeo-Christianity and Islam are called monotheistic because adherents believe their God is the one, true, and only god who wants belief in other gods suppressed—by violence, if necessary.) In modern society this idea is called multiculturalism or pluralism. Modern Western culture is pluralistic because we allow different cultures to coexist comfortably. That gay culture has arisen in such a culture is no surprise.

If the existence of gay culture offends some people's religious sensibilities, we can recognize their hostility as an indicator that their religion isn't modern enough to cope with the plurality of cultures around the world. (Here the word is just right: Nobody's got a majority, and nobody's got a right to enforce their worldview on others). This double vision can also be called multidimensionality.

The idea that some things can have more than one purpose conflicts with ancient Hebrew and biblical constructions of reality. Only one kind of grain was supposed to be grown in a field; only one kind of textile could be woven into a fabric; only one kind of food was to be eaten at a time (and only on one kind of plate). And only one kind of sex was permissible. Things had one function, and that function precluded all others (since the anus was for defecation, it was therefore not for sex). Primitive thinking allowed for only simple understanding. As humankind has evolved, we've developed a much greater sense of life's subtlety. Multifunctionality now implies richness and complexity. Morality now is not about categorizing and sorting; it's about interpersonal relations.

Joseph Campbell used to tell a story that sums up the multidimensional, polytheistic vision. During a lecture on mythology, he'd explained how the various religious traditions influenced one another, how certain doctrines developed, how the various gods around the world reflected one another, and how the gods and their followers differed from one another. In short, he'd summarized his books and the whole enterprise of comparative religion.

During the question-and-answer period after the lecture, a stern woman stood up and asserted that only one religion could be right and that all the others must therefore be false. "Mr. Campbell," she concluded, "I've been listening to you all night and...and...well, I think you're an atheist!"

"Madam," Campbell replied, "anyone who believes in as many gods as I do can hardly be called an atheist."

That kind of "not being an atheist" is precisely what the modern transformation in religion is about. The "World Religion" of the future will include all the local religions of the past without acceding to any one of them. It will offer a vision of human spirituality that makes sense of the various religions as clues to a greater truth: a deep, encompassing message about the meaning of life. (Ironically, it has been out of Islamic culture—traditionally so intensely monotheistic—that two truly global religions have already emerged: Bahá'í and the International Sufi Movement.)

This World Religion will also embrace modern Western ideals of democracy, liberty, gender equality, freedom of choice, and respect for the diversity of life. These ideals form a modern spiritual consciousness that is morally equal to all the mythologized religions that have preceded it and that have prepared humankind for it. Mature spiritual consciousness has to be big enough to include everything that went before. Being gay gives us a step up in achieving this consciousness.

Camp Humor

On a psychological level, this multidimensional double vision is apparent, for example, in the gay talent for beauty and design. Gay design is often intentionally and transparently clever precisely in its combination of unexpected elements:

antiques with '50s modern furniture, for instance, or cactus leaves and barbed wire in a wreath with Christmas balls. Multidimensional vision also informs our sense of humor. "Camp" is based on an awareness of the dual nature of everything: Things are what they are and they are also something else. The essence of irony is that what people pretend isn't what they really intend. Camp humor misdirects and exaggerates to unveil pretense. It's self-conscious and reflexive. Campiness turns things around: Inverting the old visual joke about drunks putting lamp shades on their heads, camp humor might use an outrageous ladies' hat for a lamp shade. Camp exemplifies the critical perspective of the outsider who can see there's more going on than most people realize; things aren't what they seem. The drag queen's bitchy remarks cut through the bullshit to get to the lovingly golden truth within.

Of course, in our gender blending, we must avoid the error of inadvertently eroticizing and glamorizing through campy caricature the very gender roles we're flouting and ridiculing. This "error" appears in the behavior of the gay man who parodies straight society's idea of the failed female by acting bitchy so completely that he himself becomes truly bitchy, bitter, and angry. It appears in the behavior of the butch lesbian who rejects conventional femininity and inadvertently appropriates the oppressive qualities of the straight men she imagines she's rebelling against.

Freedom from gender roles means being *natural* and naturally human, learning to be aware of feelings, and responding to others with empathy and sensitivity. It also means being unconstrained by socially determined roles.

Subject to Subject

Harry Hay, titular father of the modern gay movement, hypothesized that gay people respond to one another as subject to subject, while straight people tend to treat one another as subject to object. In other words, the nature of their sexual attraction tends to cause straight people to objectify one another, since they are attracted to a person with whom they can't identify.

We gay people are attracted to others as reflections of ourselves (but not simply in the narcissistic sense). We relate to a person we love as someone we ourselves could be. In them we see ourselves—our particular personality traits. We long for union with our beloved(s) not by producing offspring to combine our genetic patterns but by becoming *one* with them in spirit.

The heterosexual model holds that people are attracted to their "other half," their complementary opposite, to complete themselves by making the two become one. In the story in Plato's *Symposium,* human beings were originally perfect spheres that were cut in two by Zeus as punishment for hubris, each half always searching for its "other half." Except in mimicry of heterosexual jargon, gay people don't think of their partners as their other halves. (And a gay man or lesbian would never call his or her spouse "the old battle-ax.")

Men and women are taught to think differently, see the world differently, experience being in the body differently, like different movies, enjoy different smells and colors, have different priorities in life and in love, even button their shirts differently. They respond differently to sexual stimuli and respond to different stimuli. It's said there is a "war between the sexes." It's said these differences are by nature irreconcilable and should be. The differences between men and women are what draw them together to form a familial bond and to rear children who unite the couple by transforming them into parents. This duality—the ceaseless interaction of yin and yang—is what's said to keep the cosmic process going.

Homosexuals don't experience this kind of attraction. We are attracted to people like ourselves who think the way we do, who experience being in the body the way we do, and who experience sexual arousal in a similar way. What we experience as the power in relationship is harmony and congruency, not conflict and difference.

We tend to opt out of the gender identity issue by incorporating both sides in ourselves. We don't seek an opposite-gendered complement; in fact, we develop complementary qualities in ourselves by transcending gender and polarization. We look for another person who also possesses both sides.

Because we live immersed in heterosexual culture, we are raised with many heterosexual expectations. Before the era of sexual liberation, homosexuals (especially lesbians) traditionally bonded in butch-femme pairs. The development of open gay consciousness generally ended the obligatory character of that pattern. Of course, some gay people really do enjoy the differences and do experience the "opposites attract" phenomenon. Anyway, the individuals who form any couple will be different from one another. One may be older than the other, one a little butcher than the other, one more artistic or more intellectual. One may be more feeling-oriented, the other more thinking-oriented. When we see these differences through the heterosexual expectations, they may look like polarities. Even so, the differences gay people experience in their relationships are insignificant compared to the differences men and women experience in heterosexual relationship.

Being Gay Is More Basic Than Sex

Being gay is more basic than simply behaving sexually with someone of the same sex. Lots of heterosexual men, in fact, enjoy a little homosexual sex on the side. That we homosexual men have sex with other men is a consequence, not the cause, of our gayness. The cause lies in our reflection of the archetypal quality of non-duality. This is a way of seeing the world: the universe as a reflection of self, not as a complementary but different other. The grounding principle of existence is identity, not duality.

Our relationships are more symmetric than straight relationships. Homosexuals understand each other's experience of attraction. We feel the same arousal. We're attracted to each other for the same reason. We're generally attracted to the same people. We understand—and can resonate with—our partner's attraction to others because we are probably attracted to them too. (We can have three-ways.)

Straight people are compulsively drawn to individuals of the opposite sex whom they can love intensely but with whom they can never really connect. This duality creates tensions that pervade all of human culture. To be sure, it gives rise to the sexual joys of heterosexuals. It also gives rise to enmity and animosity ("You can't live with 'em and you can't live without 'em"). In a very real way, the polarization of male and female accounts for the existence of evil.

Male-Dominant Assumptions

Seeing the world with a different set of lenses helps us to see how arbitrary—and often erroneous—are many of the assumptions that most people make about the meaning of life. Male dominance, competition, hierarchy, scarcity, polarity, and the existence of good and evil are taken for granted by most people as fundamental features of human life. The reign of these assumptions determines the shape of the world we live in—all of us, gay and straight.

With the possible exception of male dominance—which the feminist movement has brought to everybody's attention as controvertible—these social conventions seem inexorable and built into the fabric of the universe. That's because the powers that champion male dominance want us all to believe they *are*. A key feature of the male sexual experience, perhaps going all the way back to our aquatic ancestors in the primordial oceans, is competition for access to females and the opportunity to father offspring. This heterosexual male struggle to reproduce gets projected onto everything and spawns many (if not all) of the problems human beings face daily. Experience of the apparent scarcity of accessible or willing females gives rise to the belief that for any kind of success in life, a host of problems must be overcome and that misfortune, injustice—and other people—stand in the way of achieving success.

We could have a world where everything everybody needed to sustain them is available and there is no scarcity and no need for competition for resources. New technologies may create a world where energy is so abundant and labor so easily automated that everything will be free. But it's unlikely the "alpha males" who've won the male dominance competition will allow this to happen anytime soon. In the meantime, we continue to believe there isn't enough happiness to go around, that we can't be generous ("If I give one to you, I'll have to give one to everybody"), that the world is fraught with problems, and that "those other people" are responsible for the problems we face. In mythic, metaphorical terms, life is an ordeal to be suffered; there's a battle between good and evil, between the sinners and the saved; and heaven must be somewhere else.

Becoming aware of how these heterosexual male assumptions color all of life is the work of spirituality and consciousness-expansion. The goal of our spiritual practice (which actually requires no achievement at all) is to see that heaven exists right here, right now, on the other side of all those dualities.

Both/And Instead of Either/Or

Conventional thinking, dominated by the influence of straight males, asserts: "I'm right and you're wrong." Nonpolarized thinking transforms that: "We're both right and we're both wrong, from different perspectives." Therefore both sides can coexist and help one another. There is no competition. This is the basis for love of neighbor and love of enemy.

This transformation demonstrates the new paradigm of "both/and instead of either/or." You can actualize this new paradigm in your daily life by practicing using the word "and" instead of "but" every time you start to say it. It's simple *and* it changes how you think.

The word *but* usually contains a lie. Here's the classic example: I want to go to the beach, *but* I have work to do. The *but* in the sentence creates the impression that these alternative ways of spending the day are contradictory and mutually exclusive. That's simply not true. The truth is that you want to go to the beach *and* you want to get your work done. Both facts are true. Making the shift in wording shows you that you might be able to adjust your schedule so you can do both. You begin to inhabit a universe full of possibilities instead of mutually exclusive alternatives.

Of course, some alternatives *are* mutually exclusive, and no amount of adjusting can change that. But if each time you start to use the word *but* you stop to consider whether you could use *and* instead, you discover there is a lot less polarization and opposition in life than we've all been taught to believe.

Non-duality allows you to avow conflicting ideas at the same time. For example, you can affirm that democracy, free enterprise, and private ownership of property are wonderful ideas *and* that Communism and collective ownership are also wonderful ideas. Both can be true. You can believe in God, and at the same time you can understand that God is a mythological image. Non-duality and multidimensionality free you from exclusivistic thinking.

Making Other People Wrong

"Making other people wrong" is an example of how polarization creates animosity and justifies enmity and misunderstanding. Making people wrong is choosing to interpret their behavior in a negative context, projecting bad faith and bad intentions onto them, assuming the worst, and judging them accordingly. It means interpreting their behavior and their motivations from the other side of a polarity, from the other side of a *but*. "I go to church on Sunday, but so-and-so plays golf" implies the golfer isn't as pious or moral as he should be and makes him wrong. "I go to church on Sunday *and* so-and-so plays golf" changes the sentence to a simple statement about various pastimes. Dropping the *but* removes the judgment by removing the opposition.

The straight world's tendency to object to gay marriage, for example, is full of *but*s. The opposition argues that recognizing gay relationships undermines and invalidates straight marriage. They look for contradiction where it doesn't exist: "They want to get married, *but* they're two men." Allowing gay people to marry doesn't have anything to do with the quality of straight marriages. There is no conflict between straight marriage and gay marriage—no scarcity of marriage licenses or conjugal bliss.

For the most part, the straight world unwittingly accepts the polarity and believes in the contradiction. They accept unthinkingly that the existence of homosexuals in the world somehow threatens the existence of heterosexuals. They see things in terms of opposing teams. They believe adversarial conflict is the best way to achieve justice.

In a very real way, straight people are always involved in a power struggle between men and women. That means, for them, that life is full of sexual possibilities and delights in overcoming the male/female opposition. It also means they are immersed in a process of polarization that gives rise to wrong-making and opposition.

Straight People Are Not the Problem

The point here is not to make straight people wrong or to criticize their behavior negatively. They are the vast majority of the human race—the normal people. There are many wonderful straight people. Indeed, there are wonderful straight *religious* people—both among our supporters and among our opponents. Obviously, most wonderful people *are* straight because most people are straight. Though the polarized worldview that heterosexuality produces remains the biggest source of the suffering and acrimony in the world, straight people are not the problem. And so we want to collaborate *with straight people* to make a better world for everybody.

Chapter 2:
How Our Homosexuality Tells Us Things

There are four ways our homosexuality tells us things: First, the very existence of homosexuality demonstrates fundamental facts about nature. Second, our actual experience of being gay causes us to discover certain truths about life and human psychology. Third, dealing with the current circumstances of gay life teaches us practical lessons about contemporary problems and issues that face us—indeed, that face all people. And fourth, there are things we find we just know though gay intuition.

These four correlate with the Jungian model of the four functions of the psyche: thinking, feeling, sensing, and intuiting. This model explains how the human mind receives information and processes it in order to achieve full experience of self and world. The aim of Jungian psychoanalysis is to bring all four functions into consciousness.

By thinking about homosexuality as an abstract reality, we arrive at a fuller understanding of sexuality. By feeling what it's like to be gay, we assess our experience and derive lessons about the nature of being human. By sensing what is going on in the world around us, we figure out how to construct a satisfying life for ourselves and for others. By intuiting, we find there are things about reality we seem to just know—as if out of the blue.

Part of the Multidimensional Fabric of Nature

The very existence of homosexuality demonstrates certain things about nature. This is why it is important that we who experience the reality of homosexual orientation champion and proclaim our perspective.

As part of the fabric of nature, found in the animal realm as well as the human, homosexuality demonstrates that life *and* sex have greater purpose than just reproduction and continuation of the species—and the status quo. There is no monolithic way to be. As Bruce Bagemihl documents in *Biological Exuberance: Animal Homosexuality and Natural Diversity,* even something as basic as sex has amazing variations. Bisexuality, hermaphroditism, transsexuality, transvestism, and of course, plain old homosexuality all abound in the animal world.

Human beings are involved in the creation of a complex ecology of consciousness. There are diverse ways to contribute to that ecology. Nature is wonderfully varied, and different people have different roles to play in its unfolding.

Accordingly, sexual pleasure and orgasm have functions other than just to induce us to pass on genetic materials. As obvious as this is, it's a revolutionary notion. Most of the rules of sexual ethics championed by the Catholic Church are based on the very opposite notion: The sole purpose of sex is procreation. In fact, outside the context of reproduction and child rearing, most of the rules of sexual behavior don't really apply. Those rules were made to create a safe environment for raising children. If there are no children, then the rules have no context.

Sexual pleasure is part of the body's self-healing, self-regulating process. Simply thinking sexual thoughts releases hormones into the blood. Orgasm changes body chemistry—you can feel it happen. It relieves stress and nurtures happiness. It helps to maintain youthful vigor. Shared with another person, orgasms deepen interpersonal bonds and perhaps, speaking mythologically, synchronize karmic patterns. Enjoying sexual pleasure is an integral part of personal development.

There is a very direct parallel with dreaming. People have long believed dreams to sometimes have religious significance; in biblical stories, God speaks through dreams. But because of their frequent sexual content, dreams have also been seen as evidence of demonic influence (by *incubi* and *succubi,* for example). Today, we understand that dreaming is an integral part of the brain's information processing. If they don't dream, human beings go crazy. Just like people need to dream, people need to have orgasm.

Sexuality and pleasure seeking aren't required by nature to be efficient. The world is full of pleasure, beauty, and extraordinary diversity. Our experience of homosexuality reminds us to relish and participate in the beauty and intensity of life. Scarcity is an illusion.

According to the principle Bruce Bagemihl calls biological exuberance, nature is wonderfully diverse, overabundant, even prodigal. Variations in sexual behavior that don't improve chances for natural selection may seem senseless and useless—indeed, sinful—in a universe of scarcity and threat, but in a universe brimming with extravagance and wastefulness, homosexuality and nonreproductive sexuality bear witness to the beneficence of biodiversity and flexibility. According to Bagemihl, diversity in social and mating systems as well as behavioral flexibility contribute positively to the evolutionary success of a species. Survival of the fittest isn't Earth's primary house rule—rather, survival of the flamboyant and exuberant. Homosexuality and sexual variance, in general, enable species to survive by increasing the range of possibilities and expanding the margins of experience.

Bagemihl cites the theory of General Economy articulated by the French philosopher, sexologist, and man of letters, Georges Bataille (who was also an important influence on gay theorist Michel Foucault). Bataille observed that there is a "superabundance of biochemical energy" bestowed freely on the planet by the sun. The challenge confronting life on Earth is not scarcity but excess. The problem is what to do with the extra energy. Nature doesn't favor efficiency, parsimony, and utility but extravagance and diversity. Life squanders life: Hundreds of baby turtles struggle to break through their eggshells and crawl down the beach to the sea, only to be eaten by predators until only a handful survive. And millions of sperm cells are expended in heterosexual mating, though only one is needed to fertilize an ovum. These observations twist conventional ideas—and male-dominance impera-tives—180 degrees. Competition isn't about the fittest win-ning but about the fittest using his prowess to stymie the reproductive opportunities of the other males. By flamboy-antly squandering reproductive opportunity, nonreproducing homosexuals assist Earth in expending excess biochemical energy. Bagemihl observes: "The equation of life turns on both prodigious fecundity and fruitless prodigality."

The opposition—Christian conservatives, for instance—generally denies the existence of homosexuality. They simply want to reduce it to contrarian behavior, not a fundamental-ly different perspective on reality. In fact, they don't like the idea that there are different perspectives at all. They don't like the idea that sexuality is such a complex force in people's lives with multiple functions in consciousness; they want to make laws to curtail its power.

Built into the lawmaking tendencies of male domination is the assumption that everybody's alike, or should be alike, and must therefore obey the same laws. These people don't think acceptance of difference is a virtue. Some Christian fun-damentalists, for example, have denounced Barney the purple dinosaur as the Antichrist because he promotes tolerance of difference. In the Christian one-way-to-heaven, Jesus-as-the-*only*-begotten-Son-of-the-Father worldview, *tolerance* and *diversity* are dirty words. You can't help wonder whether these same fundamentalists wouldn't have joined the rabble calling for crucifixion for Jesus for being soft on sinners with all that talk of his about love and forgiveness. (The play on words goes: Didn't the same vehicles that sported the bumper stickers IMPEACH BILL CLINTON also have bumper stickers that said TRY JESUS!)

The existence of homosexuality demonstrates that there are other modes of connection besides the key-in-lock/penis-in-vagina model of heterosexuality. Of course, electrical plugs fit into sockets, and the "male" end of a garden hose fits the "female" end of another hose. And of course, in some instances opposites attract and likes repel. The heterosexual consciousness sees heterosexual connections between all things. But connection also happens by reflection, by mirroring. This is connection by similarity: Like attracts like.

In fact, reflection is how consciousness itself works: In the brain, the mind creates a mirror image of what's going on outside the body in the world. Consciousness steps outside, turns around, and looks at the internal mirror image to create the experience of the world as though it were outside the body.

We'll come back to the models of connecting and find there is a topographical figure that, figuratively at least, captures the important twist that is gay connection.

As Gay, We Have Different Experiences of Life

Second, our actual experience *as gay* tells us things. Because we're homosexual, recognize it, and allow this fact to determine our choices, our lives are changed. After all, in order to identify as gay in the first place, we have to have achieved a level of self-knowledge and independence; we have to have achieved perspective on ourselves.

We live lifestyles different from the cultural norm and demonstrate the values of these alternative styles. We tend to be childless, to prize sexual adventure, to honor physical beauty, and to seek love for love's sake. Our lives prove that coupling is not just about building a nest for family, that love and sex are separable and not always at odds, and that liberation (sexual and otherwise) is a good and healthy thing. Perhaps most importantly, our experience demonstrates that you don't have to have children to lead a fulfilled life.

Childlessness is not automatically a gay trait. Many homosexuals have had children, though not as a consequence of their homosexuality. Some gay couples, especially lesbian couples, have devised ways to adopt or conceive children. Even in the recent past, it was not uncommon for homosexuals, particularly men, to marry and have children while pursuing homosexual adventures and relationships on the side. Gay identification has widened the separation between gay and straight lifestyles; gay people today are less likely to lead the double life. So the actual experience of many gay people is to be childless.

This gives us a different perspective on life. We don't have the relationship with time and aging that comes with watching one's children grow; we don't reexperience our own childhoods through our children. We don't achieve immortality by leaving progeny; we don't live on through our children and our children's children.

And we don't have the "vested interest" in the future that most parents have. We don't have to be concerned about whether things are good for our children. Which is not to say gay people are irresponsible. Living only for the moment can look irresponsible, and some irresponsible people defend their character flaws as spontaneity. But the truth is that "living for the now" is one of the major teachings of the mystical traditions. *Be here now* is a slogan not just of '60s hippies but of the ancient spiritual traditions of the East. Being here now means we can be concerned for all children, not just our own children.

We miss out on an important set of warm human feelings and activities. Yet we are blessed with one of the major mystical boons: freedom from time and the round of birth and death. Being gay untraps us in time. As spiritual writer Eckhart Tolle elaborates—with a nice gay-positive twist—in the popular New Age best-seller *The Power of Now,* to live in the Now is to find the secret to eternal life.

The point of the celibate priesthood in Roman Catholicism is that spiritual guides shouldn't have their own vested interests in the future. They should promote goodness for the benefit of all, not to influence the future for the sake of their own progeny. Single people are able to be morally driven in a way different from the experience of parents with children. Familial responsibilities create financial obligations. An oil company executive who has a wife and family to support has a stake in the status quo—and not just for himself. His self-concern is justified by his responsibilities. Thus, when a report comes across his desk about the dangers of greenhouse gases, he might be less inclined to worry about the consequences of his job for future generations in far-off countries, because of his responsibility to his own next generation. He might not quit in a fit of compunction or call upon the company to change its policies. He might disregard the concerns about the larger environment because he has his smaller environment to worry about. Of course, hopefully, he'd be concerned about the world his progeny will grow up into. But in the meantime he's got familial obligations that demand he maintain his job and not rock the boat.

As people without children, we may be much more apt to rock the boat and threaten the status quo because we're not as invested in it. We have the luxury of being able to consider whether our job is really worthwhile or fulfilling. We can open our eyes wider to let ourselves see more because our view is not blinkered by an obligation to the next generation. We have the chance to be more adventurous with our lives. We don't have to value our own genes over the welfare of other people's genes. Indeed, because we have this luxury, perhaps we also must accept it as a moral obligation.

We have different moral priorities. The rules are simply different for us. Consider sex between gay siblings or cousins: a tangential but obvious example of how basic assumptions about life are different in a homosexual context. Heterosexual sex between siblings or cousins is fraught with genetic dangers; close relatives shouldn't have offspring together. But homosexual sex play between people with these same degrees of relationship presents no such dangers. Incest isn't an issue. In fact, it's hard to imagine gay twins wouldn't have sex with each other, and adolescent sex play within the extended family—"kissing cousins"—might be much safer than with strangers (like those whom children meet over the Internet).

Of course, parent-child incest is something else entirely, or abuse by older siblings. The objection—and the danger—isn't so much genetic as psychological. Sex between people of different ages and levels of maturity, whether they're blood-related or not, always involves power, control, and personal autonomy. An important step for all children is developing a sense of autonomy and concomitant ego strength; sexual awareness is deeply tied into that. Nobody should be manipulated into sex, especially through family ties.

Another example, closer to home, is monogamy in relationship. The stability of the family is an important priority for child rearing. Monogamy and the objection to sex outside the marriage (adultery) arise from the agreement to create a family. It's about saying no to anything that threatens the nest. Outside the context of child rearing, monogamy means something different. Monogamy may be a much looser idea. Literally, monogamy—one relationship—means having "no other lover," not "no other sex." In our world monogamy is not based on the nature of the relationship itself but on the partners' needs and expectations. It's an agreement, not a law. It arises from compassion and the concern not to cause pain to one's partner. In practice this kind of monogamy may look like heterosexual monogamy, but the motivation is different. The former is based in a rule; the latter, in a feeling. The first you have to obey; the second you respond to automatically. The first is about saying no. The second requires faithfulness but offers all sorts of possibilities for mutual experience (threeways, shared sexual adventures, etc.). It's about saying yes.

We are body-oriented people. We look at others' bodies, and we look at our own bodies and think about what we look like as bodies to other people. For this reason, as young people struggling to understand the strange urges rising into our consciousness, many of us sometimes distanced ourselves from our bodies; many of us got fat, sickly, or overcerebral. We didn't feel good in our bodies. This alienation sometimes caused depression, neurosis, and damaged body image that some of us still carry. But we started to overcome this suffering in the process of coming out.

As gay, we follow the demands and urgings of our flesh. We say yes to feelings. If we did not, we would never have acknowledged our homosexuality in the first place. If ideas and ideologies meant more to us than feelings, we'd have chosen a less difficult, more socially acceptable path. We honor incarnation and attest life in the flesh a good thing. For this reason we're apt to believe in the present moment and—rather than in some fantasized afterlife that would condone a life of misery—to look for heaven on Earth.

In the Gospel of Luke (17:20), Jesus said: "The Kingdom of God is within you." The body-negative attitudes of conventional Christianity have made it seem like Jesus must have meant something ethereal and spiritual, like the Kingdom is in the mind. It makes much more sense that he meant the Kingdom of God is found in the body—in the feelings, emotions, and sensibilities that surge through the flesh and that resonate with other people as the experience of compassion. Being body-aware helps us to connect with other people empathetically.

Because we're body-oriented, we understand pain. We are less likely to cause others pain, especially out of machismo or male competition. (Gay youth never form gangs and set out to beat up straights to prove their masculinity!) People who live entirely in their minds and who deliberately ignore their bodies (and their sexual feelings) are far more likely to consider ideology more important than experience. That's how the Inquisitors and other religious zealots have historically justified torture and murder in the name of religion, believing they were doing their victims a favor.

Body awareness brings us into the present. The body lives in a much more vibrant reality than the mind, which is so caught up in analyzing and judging that it often misses the actual *experience* of being in the present. Sensing ourselves in our bodies reminds us we're alive *now.*

Besides, we are always on the spot. We may have to "come out" at any moment as we conduct our daily business. In routine interactions people may ask our spouse's name or whether we have children. Innocent questions, but they create situations in which we must either deflect the question or tell the truth. Most of the time these mini coming-out experiences are harmless. Often they're actually comforting and exciting. It's great to discover that people like you even more because you've acknowledged you're gay. They are empowered to tell you (though perhaps awkwardly) that it's OK with them. Sometimes these occasions are frightening and potentially dangerous. Coming out to the wrong person can cause a violent reaction. So we stay on edge and alert. This is alternately enlivening and anxiety-provoking.

Gay men relate to other males with a different set of criteria for evaluating them and for determining a place for them in our lives. Though we—along with the female half of the human population—might want it otherwise, straight men run the world. Accordingly, how one relates to straight men determines one's experience of the world.

Gay men first meet other men as potential sex partners. We may know there is no chance of sex happening, but we still like to hold open the possibility. That is, of course, unless he's not attractive to us. Then we're disappointed (maybe relieved) and sometimes, therefore, dismissive. If we are attracted to him, then another, much more complex set of expectations arises. These seldom come to anything; most of the men we meet in life are straight. (Though some of us are particularly prone to go after straight men. And some succeed with amazing regularity!)

For this reason we treat men as individuals, as persons with whom we could have a connection. Straight men, on the other hand, have to keep an arm's distance between themselves and all other men, especially us. They don't relate to others as individuals as easily because they must protect themselves from the possibility of homosexual connection. They tend therefore to lump people into groups and to view the world through stereotypes. That's not to say we don't also succumb to stereotypes, though ours are more likely sexual than racial, economic, or classist. Echoing Harry Hay, we see other men as subjects, not objects.

Of course, we relate to women differently too. They are not sex objects to us, not beings to be dominated. Many of us don't relate to women at all; some gay men choose to live in an all-gay world where there just aren't any women. But most of us relate well to women and sometimes form deep interpersonal bonds far stronger than those that straight men tend to form with them. We experience women as subjects, not objects. We see ourselves as their equals—if only because we're similarly marginalized by the ruling structure of society.

These same observations apply to lesbians in their relationships with other women, though lesbians' experience of sisterhood with other women is generally more profound than gay men's experience of brotherhood with other men.

All of us, gay men and lesbians, live outside the normal

connections people forge. Thus we tend to see through social protocols and to notice what's really going on. That is, we can often see how stupid, cruel, and insensitive straight men are to one another, because they're even more like that toward us. Because we're usually not in competition with them, we can see through their posturing.

We Live Amid Current Realities

Third, dealing with the current circumstances of gay life teaches us practical lessons about contemporary problems and issues that face us—and all people. Many of our discoveries about life and the universe flow directly from our being homosexual. Others flow from the situations we find ourselves in because of current religious, cultural, and political realities. Gay people don't have to be outsiders and pariahs. Cultures in the past institutionalized homosexual patterns (Greece is always the example). Today, we're not pariahs (except to the conservative religions), but we're still often cast as outsiders. As such, we see that outsiders are frequently blamed for the problems of the majority, that hate is a product of fear and neurotic projection, and that rigid gender and sex-role conventions create unhappiness and mental illness. Our experience living in contemporary, homophobia-ridden society shows us an important spiritual—and human—truth: There is no need for people to be enemies. Enmity is simply a projection of duality.

AIDS is an element of current gay life that has been tightly linked to homosexuality. Conservatives see the disease as punishment for our liberation. AIDS is supposed to make us doubt we made the right decision to accept our sexuality. But AIDS really has nothing intrinsically to do with homosexuality.

The appearance of AIDS among white gay men in the United States demonstrated that a deadly epidemic was spreading unnoticed through Africa and the rest of the Third

World (and among people of color in America and Europe).
We were the canaries in the mine, the signal that the Earth
was implementing population-cutting measures. On a human
level, the AIDS epidemic was a call for compassion.

Our experience with AIDS has shown us that sexual liberation—and modern urban crowding—demands conscien-
tiousness about hygiene. And our awareness of the importance of hygiene reveals that virulent microorganisms cause
disease, not the violation of taboos. AIDS has also taught scientists new ways of thinking about illness and treatment—
biomedical issues that are beyond the scope of this book.

But notice that AIDS has shown that the way to fight disease is to empower the immune system, not just to introduce
poisons (antibiotics) into the body in the hope that microorganisms will die before the body's own cells. That approach
has spawned microorganisms resistant to the antibiotics
through simple natural selection. As this evolutionary process
generates stronger and more virulent organisms, planet Earth
faces a new onslaught of old diseases (not to mention those
engineered by weapons manufacturers). In a way, it's been a
blessing that the first of these plagues directly affects the
immune system and has thereby promoted intense research in
this area. Because of AIDS, medicine may be much better prepared to respond to future plagues.

Dealing with the AIDS health crisis has encouraged us to
think creatively about issues of health care delivery, pharma-
ceutical drug development and experimentation, even
euthanasia and assisted suicide. It has impressed upon us the
need to reconfigure the health insurance system, which has
been predominantly based on heterosexual family ties. (One
of the goals behind the push for gay marriage/domestic part-
nership is access to employment-based health insurance, since
that's how the U.S. government has deemed American house-
holds should be covered.)

Losing friends and lovers to AIDS has given us an acute

sense of the transitory character of life. This is an important motivation for spiritual practice and concern for the greater meaning of life. The desire to understand illness, suffering, and death was the basis of Buddha's quest for enlightenment. Suffering is the business end of the spiritual demand that human beings wake up from the status quo.

The frightening inevitability of death—reinforced by every AIDS victim—is a reminder to seize the day and smell the roses. Everybody must learn these lessons; yet mainstream society keeps the lessons at bay. The warm, cuddly ideas about family and genetic immortality and the (unrealistic and unrealized) reverence for the elderly are designed to allay fears and to keep people anesthetized to painful reality. Our gay perspective at this moment in history reveals to us what most people do not want to see: All existence is transitory, and clinging to ego and normalcy won't save you.

When we understand how the mainstream media distort and confuse our issues, we have to assume that they distort and misrepresent other issues as well. Our experience as out-siders tells us that the commonly held, commonsense truths embraced by our society may not be true after all.

We also learn the unfortunate lesson that sometimes you can't trust the police. Government officials and social ser-vants who are supposed to be available to help people in need suddenly turn against us—sometimes because of their own selfish interests and perversity. The police routinely entrap innocent homosexuals by eliciting their trust, playing to their sexual attraction, and then betraying them. We can see that the police, who are supposed to represent uprightness and honesty, in fact routinely practice deceit and treachery. We learn to be skeptical of the institutions of society.

The turmoil attending our liberation forces us, individu-ally and collectively, to consider why people join the military and why there is such an institution. We're also forced to question why people marry and why there is *that* institution.

(The heterosexual joke goes: "Marriage is a great institution, but who wants to live in an institution?") We've learned that legal rights are based on participation in such institutions— participation that mainstream society takes for granted, as though everyone lives the same kind of life that hasn't changed in hundreds of years.

Gay experience over the last half century shows us that things *are* changing. We have witnessed a very dramatic and personal experience of cultural evolution. We can see first-hand how liberated our lives are compared to the lives of gay men and lesbians only one or two generations ago. We have reason to believe in progress. We, of all people, have no reason to long for the good old days. Despite the ordeal of AIDS, our gay lives are better now than they were 50 years ago. Perhaps one message of the AIDS crisis is that change and progress necessarily bring new challenges and new problems. Even so, the challenges of the present are manageable compared to the oppressive conditions of the past.

Living at this particular time in history shows us that sexual liberation relieves an enormous burden of neurosis. This is an important part of our experience as openly gay people. Consequently, we are necessarily pro-sex. When you think about how much turmoil results from sex-based neuroses, you can see how much healthier it is not to be tormented by guilt and not to be resentful or disapproving of other people's joys and styles of sexual expression.

We Know the Truth About Each Other

And fourth, there are things we find we just know by gay intuition. Many of our opinions, beliefs, shared fantasies, tastes, and styles spring from gay intuition. Some of the products of this seemingly automatic way of knowing are merely practical helps and hints: You shouldn't combine stripes and plaids, and flowers should be arranged in odd numbers of stems. Others are like urban legends and old wives' tales: We all somehow seem to get the joke about the recruitment toaster ovens! Some are special talents that simply come with being gay. Some are important. Some are frivolous (though fabulous!), like our fascination with female movie stars and our tendency to remember lines like, "I'm ready for my close-up now, Mr. DeMille."

That we share viewpoints, hold common opinions, and understand each other's humor is evidence of a gay cultural consciousness. This consciousness is characterized by an openness to novel experience, a quest for adventure, and a flare for the unusual and the queer. But the details are less important than this sense of shared consciousness, the feeling that there's a mystical, "karmic" link connecting us.

As we're growing up we train ourselves to have what society calls "women's intuition": that is, a sense of knowing things about the world and about other people. We often feel we need this kind of "second sight" to protect ourselves and our secret, even if as youngsters we don't quite know what the "secret" is. We likely find the idea of women's intuition appealing. We allow ourselves to experience this because we're not bound by gender roles like straight men. Real men, after all, don't have hunches. Men are supposed to "know," not to "have feelings" about things.

The most common manifestation of gay intuition is the phenomenon of *gaydar*. Of course, a lot of the talk about this is whimsical. It's a way to intimidate straight men by suggesting we can somehow "see" their sexual secrets. It's a way to dramatize our brotherhood by declaring we know the truth about each other. In some respects, gaydar is just projection and wishful thinking. Gay men see men they're attracted to and project mutual desire onto them. We see beauty, want it to be *our* beauty, and interpret it as a sign of shared homosexuality. But it's not always imaginary; most of the time, we're right.

Though gaydar is a frivolous notion, it absolutely dominates our lives. We spend far more time trying to figure out who else is gay than we spend actually having sex. Gaydar is the main way we experience our homosexuality moment by moment.

Gaydar seems to demonstrate two things. First, it suggests there is something so basic to homosexuality that it alters physical appearance; we're recognizable to people who know what to look for. This is certainly antithetical to the notion that homosexuality is a choice, for choices people make (like to be Catholic, or to eat meat, or not to own a television set) don't show in their visage. That we *look* gay (like people look male or female or look Negroid or Caucasoid) suggests it's something physical, natural—and very real.

Second, gaydar indicates the existence of something "supernatural," something like telepathy or clairvoyance. It is like reading other people's auras and discerning things about them that exist in their soul. Perhaps it demonstrates "karmic patterns," spiritual links between people. Our experience of gaydar shows us that people give off vibes and that we live in an environment of mind as well as of space.

All people receive vibes from other people (though not all people allow themselves to be aware of them). This isn't special to us as gay people.

But we learn to be especially attuned to the vibes people put out. We get lots of practice. We look for other delectable gay people in our surroundings—to cruise, to seek beauty to gaze upon, and to gauge the degree of our personal safety. We learn to read people's vibes to know whom we can come out to, whom we should avoid, for whom we should affect a straight, nonthreatening persona, and whom we should approach for sex.

We learn to trust other gay people. It's not that straight people can't be trusted or that *all* gay people can be trusted. Yet we feel confident that other gay people are likely to be conscientious and compassionate. At least we know they won't suddenly turn weird on us, as some straight people might if they realize we're gay. This vibe of trust is especially important in gay sexual recreation. Cruising sex partners requires us to trust our own intuition—and to trust other gay people's guilelessness. Through subtle intimations we learn with whom we can connect.

The presence of an undetectable invader—like HIV or the panoply of other sexually transmitted diseases—in gay sexual space confounds this gay intuition of safety and danger. There has been such turmoil about things like safe-sex training, disclosure of HIV status, "barebacking," and such a rift between positive and negative men—perhaps because of the "jamming" to our gaydar.

We seek affirmation in the vibes of homosexuals of the past; we like the idea that famous men and women of history were gay. And we delight in knowing something intimate about them that other—straight—people don't know. We sometimes feel a curious pleasure when we tell straight people—who are often shocked—just which famous actors, writers, or historical figures were homosexual, as though we ourselves can thereby bask in their importance and legitimacy.

Finding other attractive gay people who resonate with trust-affirming gay vibes creates a sense of a magical world around us. Gay space is safe space, secret space, and sacred space. Discovering our own homosexuality imbues the world with secrecy and magicalness.

We learn to look for signs: a hairpin dropped by another gay man to confirm our gaydar, synchronicities and coincidences, epiphanies from God. All these things tell us it's really OK to be gay and that we are beneficiaries of a special vocation that other people don't get.

The lives of those who've lived before us impart vibes that we pick up from the environment around us. This is the psychological ecology where each of us lives and finds his place in the scheme of things. We figure out who we are by examining the things that interest us and carry meaning—the vibes we resonate with.

Our homosexuality is bigger than we are; it transcends our individual existence. It is a reality we participate in, a quality of God manifesting itself in the world. Studying our experience of homosexuality reveals why we're here at this particular moment in history and how playing these particular roles serves the evolution of consciousness.

Maybe the phenomenon that we call by the cutesy term *gaydar* is the real "cause" of homosexuality. It's not that gayness is caused by biology or genetics or conditioning—all things that have to do with personhood and individuality. Maybe it's that gayness is karmic and spiritual. After all, that's what we mean when we throw up our hands at all the scientific, psychological, and political wrangling about the causes of homosexuality and say, "It's just how God made me." Maybe the "reason" we're gay is that we're resonating to gay intuition, vibrating along the gay dimensions of the spirit field. Maybe these vibes emanate from the World Mind, Gaia, or from planetary homeostasis telling the human race it's time to adjust population imperatives to the reality of life on an overcrowded, resource-exhausted planet.

That people give off vibes is a major insight into the nature of consciousness and that whole realm of phenomena called the supernatural, which is the content of religion. It explains a wide array of phenomena: ghosts and haunting, prophecy and clairvoyance, apparitions and miraculous healing, the power of prayer, mystical experience, and even UFOs and alien abductions. All are the issues of religion, the paranormal, and the supernatural.

For what we all actually are is, in Herman Hesse's words from the prologue to *Demian,* "the always significant and remarkable point at which the world's phenomena intersect." We are the intersection of genetic, historical, geographical, political, cultural, and karmic patterns. How these patterns intersect—from our DNA to the karmic vibes we resonate with—determines our particular perspective on the greater reality. That variously individuated perspective gives rise to our individual egos. And the "greater reality" is metaphorized as the Mind of God.

The major content of gay intuition is the sense of being part of a specific group and being a specific kind of person. It takes some effort to accept this intuition, but once you've done it everything else makes sense. You perceive there's a secret homosexual slant to almost everything and you see you're one of the people with the homosexual slant *because* you can recognize it. And that's the point. You see things about life and love, religion and God that other people don't see, precisely because of your gay perspective.

Chapter 3
Things Our Homosexuality Tells Us About Life

The first thing our experience of our homosexuality tells us is that we have a role to play in the unfolding of the universe. We're here for a reason, because everything is here for a reason. Everybody's experience gives him or her a reason for being, and nobody has any business discounting other people's experience.

Don't Resist Life

Our experience of homosexuality tells us the problems of homosexuals—and there are many—are not caused by homosexuality but by the bigotry of straight people (especially straight males) and, following psychologist Don Clark in the classic *Loving Someone Gay,* by our appropriation of this judgment through internalized homophobia.

Our homosexuality tells us not to be uptight about sex. Being uptight about sex, especially about male sexuality, is what causes all the problems. The lesson: Take it easy; don't resist life.

We see what is obvious to us but so difficult for straight people to recognize: Homosexuality is part of the constitutional makeup of a person, something that cannot be resisted. The tongue-in-cheek way to say this is that "Heterosexuality is much easier to change than homosexuality. Gay people just don't turn straight. But every day, all across the country, straight people turn gay!"

The various sort of "Exodus" programs that purport to cure homosexuality demonstrate that extreme guilt and neurotic religion are capable of repressing sexual desire and motivating people to perform heterosexually. This should be no surprise to anyone. The fact that so many homosexuals don't come out until adulthood, often after marrying and struggling to raise a family, demonstrates the same thing.

These "Exodus" programs actually just show that some people can repress their homosexuality and develop their heterosexuality because there really *is* such a thing as bisexuality. That only some people manage to "change" is evidence that only some people are bisexual.

But so what? It isn't as though the world needs more heterosexuals. We can see that overpopulation is *the* major problem of the world today. Why doesn't everybody see that? Aren't they paying attention? What are they resisting?

"What you resist persists" is a major notion in the spiritual/mystical traditions. But it's generally ignored by conventional religion. Male aggressive thinking naturally wants to force change (especially on other people) and to resist what isn't desirable.

Negative judgment about sex creates self-fulfilling prophecies. This is what creates the problems in the homosexual demimonde, at which the straight world points to justify its harsh negative judgment. It's a vicious, self-replicating cycle. And its basic premises are false.

Coming out, especially coming out to oneself, happens when people stop resisting the truth they know about themselves but are afraid to accept it. Coming out, therefore, teaches us one of the essential, mystical, esoteric secrets: Go with the flow; no resistance; choose things as they are. Unfortunately, this is a message many of us too easily forget. We allow the superficial demands of gay life to create the same kind of resistance that afflicted us in the straight world.

There Are Secrets

Our homosexuality reveals that there are intrigues and conspiracies going on all around us. This has been the case throughout history. There exists a secret, hidden history that in most cases can never be recovered. We can never know what's really happened, because the homosexuals involved, fearful of what heterosexuals might think of them, intended that the future never know their stories. The heterosexuals who did know may have colluded in the secret by destroying evidence after a person's death "to protect his reputation." As gay, then, we understand there have always been sexual and homosexual motivations, intrigues, and conspiracies behind the events of history.

Different Reasons for Living and for Working

Gay people experience different reasons for living and for working. We don't live to give birth to offspring, and we don't take a job in order to build a nest for those children. We don't have to be trapped in the conventional world in order to fulfill parental responsibilities.

Childless and relatively independent of the siblings and cousins that make up family, we demonstrate how to live and grow old without having a family to take care of us or children who have to love us. In a world of broken marriages, serial divorce, dysfunctional families, and single parents, our example is a lesson for the nongay world.

We form enduring friendship circles and so-called intentional families. We form bonds with people because we want to, not because we have to.

One of the most tragic things about the AIDS epidemic has been its toll on the networks of friendship. The disease has decimated crowds of friends who thought they would live their whole lives together as companions and partners of all sorts. At the same time, those deaths have strengthened these circles and energized them to provide the kind of support and solace required by tragedy and collective grief. Certainly AIDS has demonstrated how people can come together across family lines.

Because of oppression and homophobia in society, we are likely to seek jobs that don't expose us to threats of being fired for our gayness. Gay people often choose to be self-employed and/or enter certain professions—hairdresser, florist, or designer—that both protect them from harassment and nourish their inherent skills and talents. Also among those talents are interpersonal skills and sensitivity to others. Hence gay people make good nurses, doctors, teachers, and social workers. These are jobs in which the blending of mas-culinity and femininity imparts special abilities.

A single nonparent works for reasons different than a parent with responsibilities to his or her children. Gay people can choose to work at a job because they enjoy it. And they can demonstrate to nongay people that it's possible to enjoy one's job (something many mainstream people never experi-ence and cannot accept). As we saw earlier, we have the lux-ury, privilege, *and responsibility* to practice what the Buddhists call Right Livelihood.

Gay people can choose a job because it allows them to make a contribution to the world, not just because they have to have a job and an income in order to fulfill parental responsibilities. Of course, in reality, regardless of our sexual liberation and enlightenment, we may have to take a job whether we like it or not, because we need the money.

But we see the point of work is to have a good time. Indeed, the point of *life* is to have a good time. This is a sig-nificant shift from a traditional (Protestant) view of life as an ordeal to undergo in order to fulfill one's duties and thereby to earn a reward in an afterlife. You can see how having a good time could get in the way of being a responsible parent.

Thus you can see how religious authorities might have wanted to shift the emphasis in order to make sure everybody was a good parent. Besides, a main function of orthodoxy has been to keep the workers and soldiers in line so they don't question why the rich and powerful enjoy such luxuries or why they have to labor and risk their lives to maintain those alpha males at the top. Many religious traditions include an elaborate indoctrination in the belief that life is a vale of sorrows where people shouldn't expect to have a good time. Unfortunately, this becomes another self-fulfilling prophecy.

If everybody believed life should be a joy, a lot of jobs just wouldn't get filled. Maybe we'd all have to take turns being cesspool cleaners, for instance. The idea that we could negotiate how to get the "bad," lower-caste jobs done (like harvesting the sugarcane in Cuba) is forbidden by the conventions of male domination. In modern America this idea has been called "communist" and presented as ungodly, even though it is a logical extension of participatory democracy, egalitarianism, and Christian charity.

The "family values" people oppose gay rights just because people who are gay (in the political sense of the word) appear to be too gay (in the etymological sense). Living the myths of competition and scarcity means that for some people to be on top, other people have to be on the bottom: "I can't be happy if everybody else is happy."

The purpose of life is to experience joy *in the immediate moment.* As we've been seeing, this is an important notion in all the world's philosophical *and* mystical traditions: live in the present, "smell the roses," *carpe diem,* be here now.

This is advice for everybody, of course. And we gay people must remind ourselves of its wisdom just as vigilantly as straights, since we all live in a world focused on past and future. But because we usually don't have children, we're less concerned with the passing of time and the achievement of immortality through offspring. It is easier for us to follow this advice. Besides, our sexual freedom often prompts us to seize opportunity, with less regard for future consequences. (This, of course, creates a whole set of problems in gay culture; unsafe sex is just one of them.)

Gender Arrangements Are Arbitrary

People see what they expect to see. They don't see objectively but through filters they've acquired through their culture and their experience. And they generally are not aware of the filters. When we look out at the world, we assume that's "just the way things are."

Straight people see a straight world. The ethical principles based on heterosexual experience appear absolute, just as the problems resulting from them appear inevitable. Stepping outside the straight worldview, we perceive solutions to some of the problems just by changing the assumptions.

Politicians polarize the electorate. They become committed to their platforms rather than to solving problems. In fact, politicians' polarization into competing parties sometimes prevents them from participating in problem solving if compromise aids the other side. By making the other side wrong, they think they're making themselves right. But the important thing isn't being right; it's getting the job done. Both sides could recognize the problems, try different solutions, and test them for their effectiveness. It shouldn't matter who "wins."

We've seen that many of the problems that bedevil modern society arise from the rigid gender-role conditioning human beings have inherited from earlier times when (maybe) they made sense. Gender conditioning is just too limiting. It doesn't work in a modern, psychologically aware, egalitarian society. The male-dominated social order evolved with agrarianism, the need to organize workers to keep the food supply steady, and the need to raise armies to protect the homeland. We've evolved long past these imperatives, but the roles haven't changed accordingly. The male-dominated social order now promotes violence and oppression as often as good order. It doesn't support the creation of world peace, harmony, or human fulfillment.

The gender arrangements we now follow and that most people accept—even though they are not necessarily satisfying—are not the only options. The rise of gay consciousness illuminates other ways of experiencing self, body, and place. What a new emotionally and psychologically satisfying relationship between men and women—and between gay and straight people, of course—will look like is hard to guess.

Gay people's experience does give everybody some guidance. We know it's better not to be driven by fear and that finding your true self requires self-examination and liberation from parental and societal expectations. Masculinity and femininity need not be mutually exclusive or contrary. Right and wrong are social constructs. Live in the present, pursue your heart, and follow your bliss.

In all likelihood our current psychological awareness of personality structure and mental function will result in a devaluing of male aggression and competitiveness and in a greater esteem for women's assertiveness, creativity, and independence. In the long run, technological development is most likely to change gender-role conditioning. An absolutely abundant supply of energy—from controlled nuclear fusion, superefficient solar cells, or something we can't even presently conceive of—would eliminate the myth of scarcity that justifies class and economic difference. When everything is free everybody can be rich. That's what we should all intend for the future.

The goal of the gender roles we inherited from the development of agrarianism was to expand the population, to provide food for the growing numbers of mouths, and to exert male dominance. When everybody is equal the gender roles will no longer serve any useful function. Changing gender-role conditioning and helping people to be happier and more fulfilled has to result in a reduction of global population.

Being Straight Vs. Being Heterosexual

Being straight and being heterosexual are not the same thing. And in fact, the need to be straight can seriously diminish a man's ability to respond honestly to his true heterosexual impulses. Being straight is about conforming to the rigid sex and gender roles that say men are supposed to dominate women and women are supposed to be submissive to men. Being straight is about a man's not being like a woman. So straight men are often more strongly driven by the need to *look* straight to themselves and to other men than they are by their actual heterosexual feelings.

Regardless of his true inclination, a man may have to fuck a woman simply because she's there because not acting on sexual possibility conflicts with being a "real man." And he may not be able to tell her he loves her and is dependent on her, when in fact he is desperately attracted emotionally and sexually. Men are sometimes driven more by other men's opinions than by concern for their relationship with women. This is exemplified in the classic frat boy compulsion to brag about sex (even when it didn't happen) and to reduce women to scores in a game with fraternity brothers.

Of course, gay men sometimes also have sex in order to prove to themselves and other men that they are real men, but the gay version of the compulsion likely includes the need to be desired by the other. This makes the sexual connection more complicated and demands that each man be vulnerable to the other—emotionally submissive, if not physically so. A gay man's desire for sex is established early in life, when the desire for sexual connection is about discovering that he is not alone and that there really are other homosexuals. What better proof of that than finding another man who wants sex with you as much as you want it with him?

The point is that people should respond to their deepest sexual and emotional urges, not to societal expectations. Truth comes from personal experience, not obedience to authority or convention.

Projection and the Shadow

Homophobia and gay oppression are examples of the dynamic of projection and the archetype of the Shadow. These ideas in psychoanalytic theory derive specifically from the work of Carl Jung, but they have become part of every-day speech. Our awareness of these dynamics is major evidence of modern psychological sophistication; 100 years ago people couldn't have even thought about them. That we can—even if not always correctly—signals how different we moderns are from our ancestors and how dramatically the psychological world has changed. And all because human beings developed the ability to step outside themselves and look at their behavior from an outsider's perspective.

The notion of projection says that how we see the world is influenced by our past experiences, presumptions, and indoctrination. We tend to understand things in the present by associating them with things we've learned or experienced in the past. We see through our filters, but we tend not to see the filters. Instead we perceive the memories, associations, and assumptions as though they were actually the things in the present. We project them onto other people and configure them as part of the other rather than as part of ourselves.

If a vicious dog frightened you when you were a child, as an adult you're likely to be wary of dogs. When you see a big dog, you're reminded of your childhood experience, and you project that experience onto the dog in the present. Instead of thinking "Here comes a dog; I remember once having a bad experience with a dog; I better be watchful," you're more apt to see the dog coming toward you and then interpret the dog's actions as signs of its viciousness without ever recollecting your childhood experience. The trauma moves right through you onto the dog. Sometimes this projection can even become a self-fulfilling prophecy: Your reaction to the dog might actually frighten the dog, so it reacts defensively, thus "proving" you weren't projecting. The dog *was* vicious.

Conversely, if as a child you had a wonderful experience playing one afternoon with a red cocker spaniel, 20 years later you might—unconsciously—associate the lovely red hair of a handsome man you've just met with the joy of that childhood afternoon and "fall in love." He may not be who you imagine him to be at all. Early in the developing relationship, it will be important to see what's projection and what's real in your perception of him. This is how infatuation becomes love.

Projection is a good word for this because it reminds us of movie theaters. We all know the movie is a series of images on a strip of film a couple of inches wide and that the image on the screen is projected by a machine at the back of the theater behind a wall with a little window. When you look back, you can see the light flickering and jumping about through that little window. But moments after the movie starts, you forget that entirely. The "movie" isn't the coil of film; it's the world 20 feet across on the screen in front of you. Indeed, as soon as the opening credits end, you might even forget it is a movie. It becomes a world.

That's exactly how we project past memories into the world around us. But the screen isn't a silvery panel—it's other people. Sometimes we are conscious that we're seeing the world through the "light" we're projecting onto it, like in the theater. But most of the time the subject matter is so important (even important to our very survival) and so demanding that we believe our projection is really the world.

One set of associations the mind routinely makes is to

previous experiences of pain and fear. These have been major events that have shaped us. Actually, *all* associations are to experiences of pain, fear, and threat to survival because all associations chain backward to infancy and birth, when survival was the *only* issue. So all associations are with survival anxiety. Only in our mother's arms were we secure, and at any moment she was likely to lay us back in our crib alone—and fearful of abandonment. We are liable to fear abandonment our entire lives and to project that fear into the world as threats to our survival. This mechanism keeps us enthralled by the projection and hinders our ability to see beyond it.

Jungian ideas have been applied to the case of gay men by gay psychotherapist and theorist Mitch Walker, one of the progenitors of the Radical Faerie movement, especially the idea of the Shadow. The phenomenon Jung called the Shadow is the unconscious tendency humans all share to see our own upsetting and traumatic "stuff" in the world around us. There is stuff about ourselves we've learned not to see; traits in ourselves we don't like, don't want to know about, and certainly don't want others to know about. These traits get pushed into the Shadow—into parts of ourselves we *can't* see because there's no "light," no awareness there. In fact, we project these traits out onto other people in order to not acknowledge them in ourselves. We see our own worst habits in the behavior of others and, fearing they threaten our very survival, we react with disapproval and defensiveness.

The way to find out what you don't like about yourself is to see what you *really* don't like about other people. You're likely to react especially intensely and compulsively when the traits you don't like in somebody else correspond to your own Shadow projected onto them. Of course, sometimes people really do possess annoying traits; it's not always your imagination. But the fact that you're particularly bothered by those traits is a sign that they're part of your Shadow.

Even when you repress bothersome traits in yourself, all

you've really accomplished is to keep yourself in the dark about them. You may still act them out. Other people may still see them and respond or react to them. Of course, other people project onto you too and react as much to their own stuff as to yours.

According to Jungian theory, the Shadow can be a great boon. It's the opportunity to see things in your own mind that you aren't letting into consciousness. Since psychoanalytic theory highly values self-knowledge as liberating and enlightening, the things that especially bother you in other people are the things you want to be aware of in yourself. The goal isn't necessarily to begin to act out the suppressed traits; rather, it's to know why you suppress them and to not be compulsively bothered by them in others.

Scapegoats

Virulent opposition to gay people is a dramatic demonstration of how repressed traits and behaviors are projected outward onto other people, who become scapegoats. People are most likely to suppress their tendencies for violating gender-role conditioning. After all, the imperatives of male domination aren't really conducive to happiness—though this is something nobody is ever supposed to say out loud. Conditioning is inculcated through fear, terror, and threat.

People who have been conditioned very well don't know they've been conditioned (that's part of the conditioning), and they don't like anything in themselves that seems even slightly irregular. A man therefore might feel uncomfortable with his own desire to relax and not be competitive. He might feel less manly. He worries that he is lazy (instead of friendly). And he finds laziness particularly upsetting in other people. He might, for example, believe that people who suffer financial setbacks and end up on welfare are really lazy and don't deserve government assistance. He's especially strident about his beliefs when he considers the possibility that he might suffer financial reversals himself. The more aware he is of insecurity and financial volatility (in a system designed to produce volatility so there can be winners and losers), the more upset he is when other people need financial assistance. He might even blame the poor (and taxes that have to be levied to assist them) for his own financial worries. And that's just about money. The stakes are even higher when projection is about sex, the real issue of gender-role conditioning!

Straight men project their failings to live up to an impossibly difficult standard of masculinity onto women and homosexuals. A man who doubts his ability to perform sexually might project his anxiety onto his wife. It's her fault he can't stay hard, so he beats her up to prove he's a real man. His inability to have a loving, satisfying relationship with his wife is the fault of homosexuals; because they want to marry, his marriage is on the rocks!

Gay men are damned for being promiscuous. The universal human desire for pleasure and sexual expression gets repressed by the notion that sex is dirty (at least when other people do it) and by the realities of day-to-day married life. It's all complicated by the straight male's belief that no one should be having more sex than he is, that "real men" get all the sex they want, and that he's not a real man if his desires aren't satisfied. No wonder sex isn't ultimately fulfilling! When sex doesn't bring the perfect fulfillment promised by the gender conditioning, straight men project onto homosexuals all the unruly and illicit urges that in a rigidly controlled situation they naturally feel. Because our subcultural institutions for connecting sexually are all most people know about our culture, they assume all we ever do is have sex. That's not so, of course, but it is nice we have institutions, like gay bars and sex clubs, that do allow us to meet and to breathe the gay air.

Straight men worry that if they are in a bathroom or shower with a gay man, they are liable to be hit on. They assume all gay men want to take them sexually, because that's how they feel about women. This is the classic problem for the military: the cliché about dropping the soap in the shower. Straight men project onto gay men their desire for sex with all women.

The assumption is that straight men are sexually attracted to women just because they're female and not necessarily because of who they are or what they look like. Stereotypically, straight males will have sex with any available female just because she is there. That's why males and females have to be kept separate in bathrooms and changing rooms. People assume that a woman, regardless of whether she's a beauty, would be taken sexually if she undressed in a locker room full of straight men. Straight men are driven by *female-ness* itself. Women have to practice sexual selection and, there-fore, become the object of males' disappointment and anger if they reject them.

In fact, gay men aren't like that. Of course, there are set-tings, like public tearooms, where gay men go to have sex with virtually anyone and everyone, if possible. But most gay settings are not like that. All the men in a gay bar, for exam-ple, are potentially available to each other. That's why they are there. But most of the men don't connect; availability itself isn't enough. There has to be sexual attraction, a deep compulsion to connect, or a vibe. This is the source of endless feelings of rejection for us. We are selective, in part, out of our idealism and our longing to find true love.

Women—and gay men—are selective. It's because of the selectivity of the women in a straight bar that not all the men get laid. The soap-in-the-shower argument against gays in the military is ludicrous because we know we wouldn't be attracted to a man just because he was there. It would take more than that to get us interested. Of course, sometimes there is something there to get us interested; gay men *are* eas-ily interested. But the interest seldom means forcing sex. The interest wants to be reciprocated.

Homosexuals are blamed for child molestation and the breakdown of the family. Husbands and wives, perhaps no longer sexually attracted to one another because they've come to resemble their own parents, may feel turned on by the blossoming sexual allure of their own children. In their children they see their youthful selves or the young girl or young man they fell in love with in their own youth. Parents' sexual awareness of their own children tweaks the incest taboo, whereupon they repress this anxiety into unconsciousness and project it outward onto homosexuals, who seem so alien and whose sex it makes them compulsively upset even to think about. We gay people all know child molestation is a predominantly straight phenomenon; the statistics bear this out. But the cultural projection is that homosexuals are child molesters, an error in perception that dominates social (and church) policy.

The real threat to the family is heterosexuals' loss of sexual interest when they shift from being sexually active youths to being parents. Marriage threatens sex; living in the isolated nuclear family puts enormous stress on husbands and wives to be everything for one another. The so-called breakdown of the family gets blamed on homosexuals, who don't have to become parents and can therefore remain sexually playful. Passing laws to prevent recognition of gay marriage does nothing to address the stresses of traditional heterosexual marriage. In fact, by misdirecting public consciousness, legislation probably exacerbates the problems.

Competition and Winner-Take-All

Because other male animals compete with each other for access to females, we assume competition and possessiveness are also fundamental human experiences. Perhaps they are simply heterosexual experiences. Gay men's sexual activity is often about joining, not excluding.

The male competition supports the erroneous ideas that life is a test, that the reward for success comes in the afterlife, and that others' suffering is of no consequence because it will be corrected in that afterlife. This foolhardy esteem of hierarchy and competition promotes a winner-take-all mentality that makes cooperation and harmony hard to achieve.

One of the most serious global problems is misallocation of resources. A few people control most of the natural and economic goods. In consequence, the great majority of people are left out. We see this phenomenon in the arts, sports, literature—and in gambling. Lotteries are a prime example. The prize for guessing a winning series of numbers in a government-run lotto game can be as high as $150 million. That's more than anyone could spend in several lifetimes. Giving each of 150 winners a million dollars would make more sense; the money would help more people and help them more realistically. However, the phenomenon of lotto fever indicates that the public is more interested in games when the prize is enormous and the chances of winning are slimmest.

A few famous sports figures and movie stars are paid phenomenal sums, while most people who struggle to be a part of the sports and entertainment business don't make enough money to maintain a career. Big New York publishing companies prefer a single book that sells millions of copies to hundreds of books that sell only a few thousand copies apiece. Hundreds of worthy manuscripts will be rejected. Diversity is lost and opportunities squandered because of the winner-take-all, competition-based mentality.

The winner-take-all mentality creates the problem in gay life of looksism. The most beautiful men get all the attention and the less beautiful feel inadequate and left out. This doesn't make life better for those at the top; pretty people are just as apt to suffer body image anxiety, to worry about what other people think. What we all really want is all of us sharing ourselves without the obsession with hierarchy, with winning the hottest guy. As gay people, with a certain consciousness of what's going on, we can declare we don't want to get stressed out about competition. We should know not to worry about what other people think.

Gay Men Aren't Warlike

Because of our ability to encompass both male and female gender traits, gay men aren't usually interested in violence. We get queasy at the thought of somebody getting hurt. Most of us don't even like sports because there's too much violence, too much competition. Many of us like "chick flicks" because they stir feelings. We might go see a shoot-'em-up movie with a hot macho movie star, but we likely chose the movie because the trailers showed the star with his shirt off than because we wanted to get a dose of violence and mayhem. We aren't warlike.

Of course, there are gay men who go to fight in wars, and their right to be in the military is a *cause célèbre* of the movement. But the gays-in-the-military issue is not evidence of homosexual belligerence. People are motivated to join the military as much to be of service and to be part of something bigger than themselves as to engage in masculine violence.

The soap-in-the-shower scenario gives rise to the fallacy that homosexuals want to join the military so they can prey on young heterosexual innocents, recruiting and perverting them during their time of separation from a mixed-sex environment. The truth is that idealistic, service-motivated, young homosexual innocents—sexually unaware or struggling to suppress sexuality through patriotism—join the military for all the best reasons. Military discipline, after all, is presented as a normalizing experience: Bad boys, screwed-up kids, and social misfits can be saved at military school, in the Boy Scouts, or in the Army. (Or they can go to seminary.) It's then within the same-sex environment that they discover their sexuality. Military service is traditionally one of the ways homosexuals have their eyes opened to the reality of same-sex attraction. (There's a good argument that modern gay consciousness had its beginnings in the world wars, when military service introduced many young men to sexual possibilities they'd never before considered.)

The objection to gays in the military is that we foul up unit cohesion. That's because we don't share straight men's belligerence, sexual bravado, and anger toward women. The presence of polite, sensitive men spoils the fun of the macho warriors. At least in part, that's what "damaging to unit cohesion" means: Boys can't be boys when there's somebody around who knows how to act like an adult.

Humans have two evolutionary siblings: chimpanzees and bonobos. These two jungle-dwelling primates look similar—like Bonzo, the movie chimp—though bonobos are a little prettier, cuter, and have better hair. But the two primate cultures are totally different.

Chimps are violent. Males beat their females. The males fight with each other in sport and competition, and fight over access to females. They kill other animals for food. Chimps display rigid sexual behavior patterns and practice male sexual ownership of females. Males even enforce this "monogamy" by killing the offspring sired by other males.

Bonobos, on the other hand, are promiscuous and routinely have sex both heterosexually and homosexually. Males don't possess females: no monogamy and no enforced heterosexuality. Their society is matriarchal—females run things, not males. And bonobos are nonviolent. Their males don't fight with each other or with females. They are mostly vegetarian.

In metaphorical terms, perhaps the bonobos represent the inhabitants of Eden who tarried in paradise after "men" committed the original sin: thinking sex bad and shameful, and violence and competition admirable. Perhaps the universe prizes pleasure and rewards those who generate it with peace and love. If we think this idea sounds strange, we betray the degree to which our religious attitudes are bound by the chimpanzee traits we've inherited.

Of course, humans aren't apes anymore, and ape behavior doesn't prove anything about human behavior. But doesn't the difference between chimp and bonobo culture suggest that liberation from sex rules might be the cure to violence? And doesn't this difference resemble the contrast between straight and gay culture?

In the language of mythology, we have to wonder whether good bonobos get reincarnated as gay men—or, conversely, whether good gay men get reincarnated as bonobos!

Terror

As gay people, we have been living with terror and the threat of violence all our lives. The homophobia in our society threatens suddenly to appear in the form of Christian missionaries who harangue us with Bible verses, gay-baiters, bullies, or murderers. The killing of gay people, especially young men, is an act of terrorism. Like all acts of terror, this form of violence is intended to send a message to others in the targeted group. Young straight men attack gay men because they're reminded of their own fluid sexuality. They want to scare people back into the closet to reduce their own anxiety.

The reluctance of state and federal legislators to adopt hate-crimes bills only adds to the terror. Government officials say, in effect, they don't think gay bashing is something that needs to be stopped the way religious or racial attacks need to be stopped. Outlawing antigay hate is considered an endorsement of the gay lifestyle. Conservative politicians agree that homosexuals ought to respond to threats against them by staying in the closet; it's our own fault if we're attacked.

Ironically, we also have experience being terrorists. Our very presence seems to strike fear into the hearts of certain straight men. Our forthrightness threatens their security. We outrage them.

The gay political movement has sometimes used this ability to strike terror for political advantage. These "zaps" have taken many forms over the decades. In the years following Stonewall, gay activists in New York (some of them, incidentally, under the leadership of gay philosopher and progenitor of Faerie spirituality, Arthur Evans) attended public events like the 100th anniversary of the Metropolitan Museum of Art or the opening night of the opera's new season. These were places where politicians were out to be seen and to shake hands. However, when the activists got hold of the politicians' hands, they didn't let go. "When are you going to speak out on homosexual rights?" they asked, hanging on until the police dragged them away. The politicians turned to the next face in the crowd, only to have the same thing happen and the same question repeated: "When are you going to speak out on homosexual rights?" A decade and a half later, to protest the government's silence about AIDS, ACT UPers blocked the Golden Gate Bridge in San Francisco and disrupted Mass at Saint Patrick's Cathedral in New York.

This was "terrorism" in the service of humanity. The purposes of social action should always be to wake people up to injustice and suffering as well as to present grievances for redress without causing physical harm. Terror has to have specific, accomplishable goals and the promise of an end. If the perpetrators can't stop the violence, the frightened victims have no motivation to respond to their demands and can only retaliate in kind.

As oppressed victims ourselves, we see that, however misguided, terrorists take some worthy ideal as their touchstone and think they're doing right. But we also see how terrorism usually goes wrong. The attacks on the United States in 2001 mainly resulted in military retaliation, American outrage, and the destruction of Islamic societies. The attacks did nothing to redress the terrorists' original grievances.

The correct use of force is always the least amount leveraged to create the greatest effect. Arthur C. Clarke observed that it's the proper application of power that matters, not its amount. How long, he asked, would the career of a Hitler have lasted if wherever he went a voice was talking quietly in his ear? Or if a steady musical note, loud enough to drown all other sounds and prevent sleep, filled his brain day and night?

With all the money and brainpower that has gone into creating the world's nuclear arsenals—weapons we dare not use—couldn't such a system have been invented that targeted individuals (a Pol Pot, a bin Laden, or a Saddam Hussein) instead of national populations? Why do weapons have to be destructive? Couldn't the tyrant be rendered euphoric with a ray or a chemical so that he'd joyfully relinquish power? Indeed, why should chemical weapons have to be toxins? What if instead of nerve gas, clouds of aerosolized ecstasy could be sent rolling rapturously over an offending army so that the soldiers surrendered happily and amorously? Male domination imperatives of competition, anger, revenge, and retaliation result in the misapplication of power and the horrors of modern warfare, and delay effective, nonviolent strategies for global peace.

Pleasure Is Good

Pleasure is good in itself. It is participation in the flow of life—you can feel that. The whole body is wired for pleasure. No kind of bodily pleasure is obscene.

The desire for pleasure doesn't cause people to do bad things. People do bad things because of anger, greed, hatred, animosity, envy, resentment, disapproval, and violence—all of which a little pleasure might help to relieve! Orgasm releases destructive feelings. In a very real way, it's like electroshock therapy, only better—and more natural. Orgasm is good for the soul. The desire for pleasure makes some people cunning, manipulative, and neurotic. But even in these instances it's not the pleasure that warps them; rather, it's the frustration of the desire for pleasure. Orgasm is part of the body/mind's self-healing.

Pleasure happens in the flesh. Religions worldwide have an ambivalent relationship with the flesh. This shouldn't surprise us. The experience of suffering inspired the creation of religion, and suffering happens in the flesh. The subtle, ongoing suffering we all endure—aging and eventual death—is the direct consequence of incarnation. And the demands of flesh for food, shelter, and comfort give rise to the need to toil.

According to Saint Thomas Aquinas, for centuries the "official" theologian of the Catholic Church, the stain and the consequences of original sin—suffering and death, the pain of childbirth, and the obligation to toil—are transferred to a newly conceived soul by the parents' orgasm(s) that resulted in fertilization. In other words, in the orthodox Catholic view orgasm is the cause of all evil.

Everyone in the premodern world was constantly faced with disease, dirt, and the need for endless toil. Farming was hard work. Housekeeping was hard work. Preparing food was hard work. There was virtually no way of getting anything completely clean. Sanitation as we know it in the modern world just didn't exist. *Living* was hard work.

Religion promised a reality beyond the suffering, toil, and dirt of life. To get people to accept that "supernatural" reality, the purveyors of religious myths disparaged the concept of too much awareness or preoccupation with the concerns of the body. (We all understand that if we were allowed to experience pleasure constantly, to live in a state of continuous orgasm, we wouldn't do anything else. "Why did God create ejaculation?" the joke goes. "So gay men would know when to stop.")

Another reason religious authorities sought to control people's desires for physical pleasure was to maintain the line of genealogy and inheritance. Heterosexual sexual pleasure can result in pregnancy, and premodern cultures had a major social interest in regulating pregnancy. As we've seen, men had to compete for access to females—for the opportunity to pass on their name and their genetic line. The desire for pleasure could easily cloud people's minds and cause them to do things that might upset the social order. And indulgence in sexual pleasure sometimes produced strange afflictions that seemed like punishments from God. (Many cases of "leprosy" described in Scripture and other ancient texts were likely syphilis.)

We use the word *pleasure* in two ways: sex and comfort. Pleasure is the physical sensation and alteration of consciousness that come with sexual arousal. Pleasure is also relief from the effort that life demands. Religion promised an escape from suffering and toil by disparaging the desires of the flesh. This worldview also served to maintain social order by keeping the lower classes at work so the upper classes (sometimes including the priests) were free from the burdens of life in a body.

The modern world has a totally different relationship to the flesh. Daily bathing, indoor plumbing with hot and cold running water, soap, antiseptics, toothbrushes, deodorant, toilet paper, tampons, and condoms have radically changed our experience of hygiene. They've also distanced us from the physical world. Many of us who live in cities go for days without coming into contact with anything natural or earthy. Our food comes wrapped in plastic film. We defecate in white porcelain bowls and flush away our bodily wastes without ever looking at them. We seldom see death. We barely know we're incarnated in dirty, mortal flesh. One could argue that we've gone too far in the other direction, escaped flesh another way.

The Golden World

Our attitudes about pleasure should be positive instead of negative. Body and soul aren't at odds. For our mental health and spiritual well-being, we need to rediscover pleasure—our connection to the organic world—lest we lose touch with our place in Earth's ecology and go mad in our sterile ivory towers.

In the premodern worldview espoused by religion, there was an Edenic Golden Age sometime in the past from which human beings "fell" because of sin, uncleanness, and desire. Salvation from the Fall came when one turned away from the fallen world, obeyed religious injunctions about ritual and sexual purity, and anticipated a return to the Golden World in a spiritualized afterlife. In that worldview, to allow yourself to feel pleasure was to succumb to sensuality and materialism, and risk losing salvation.

The modern worldview, based on science and reality, understands that the Golden World is a metaphor for mystical vision and for future possibility. Eden lies in the future, not the past. (Actually, Eden is in the present.) The world of incarnation need not be a vale of suffering. It is, instead, the opportunity for evolution. The modern worldview perceives life on Earth to be developing from less consciousness to more consciousness; the spiritual, "New Age" side of this worldview says this mythologically: Life is evolving into God. Evolution happens at the interface between body and mind. Change happens in the form of the flesh, which in turn affects consciousness. Sex is part of that process. The desire for sexual pleasure, after all, motivates humans' participation in evolution.

Pleasure is found within you—just like the Kingdom of God. The error of so-called materialism isn't that it is focused on pleasure and sensuality but that it looks for pleasure and satisfaction in the outside world. Materialism and sensuality are actually opposites. Sensuality isn't about things; it's about being aware of feelings, emotions, and bodily sensations in the moment. Materialism is a male-dominance trait, a manly response to the problems of life, consistent with the assumptions of hierarchy, scarcity, and competition. Materialism is about mind-stuff: judgment, comparison, sovereignty, respect, and authority. It's not about being in the body. It's about escaping the body and the world of women, where feelings and emotions—things experienced in the body—reign.

Taking pleasure in the flesh is not a descent into the fallen world. Quite the opposite: The experience of pleasure has beneficial and health-giving effects—the endorphins and neurotransmitters associated with feeling pleasure are good for the body and the mind. Pleasure helps us grow. If we understand it properly, pleasure helps us evolve.

The notion that what people do for pleasure is selfish and worthless, that pleasure is a tug away from spirituality into gross materiality, is just another example of dualistic thinking.

Chapter 4
Things Our Homosexuality Tells Us About Sex

The Tantric and Taoist traditions in the East devised techniques for generating mystical experience out of sexual pleasure. Under a variety of names these traditions have resurfaced in modern—especially New Age—thinking. In the gay men's world this phenomenon is best known through workshops called Celebrating the Body Erotic. These workshops were originally created by a gay former Jesuit, Joseph Kramer, and organized under the auspices of the Body Electric school of massage in Oakland, Calif.

Body Electric trains participants to expand their experience of physicality and sexuality, to rethink their socially and religiously conditioned ideas about arousal and self-pleasuring, and to discover that prolonged arousal generalized throughout the body "charges" them with erotic energy. This buildup of erotic charge can effect personality-transforming changes in consciousness, perhaps health-giving changes in the body, and even produce mystical and transcendent experiences.

The high point of the Body Electric training is receiving—and, in turn, giving—a prolonged erotic massage. During this massage the receiver practices a shallow, circular breathing technique that alters his blood chemistry so that ejaculation is virtually impossible. Following well-choreographed instructions from the trainer, the giver strokes the receiver's penis with one hand to generate sexual energy and with the other massages and caresses him to move the energy throughout his whole physique but not release it. The massage ends with "the big draw": The receiver takes several long, deep breaths, then clenches all the muscles in his body as long as he possibly can, then suddenly relaxes. In an abrupt release of energy, he throws his arms and legs wide open, sending the erotic charge up through his consciousness and into mystical space.

Sex as Prayer

When we understand pleasure as the affirmation of life and sacralization of the shared reality, we transform pleasure. Of course, there are people who can't control their urges (who do indeed spend all their time masturbating), but for most people pleasure is a good thing that doesn't create problems. And gay experience shows us that pleasure and sex don't have to be justified by having babies (and thereby adding to one's toil). Honoring pleasure—proudly wanting to experience it for oneself and generously wanting other people to experience it joyously for themselves—brings consciousness into the real world, where we can do something to save the planet and to bring on the evolution of spirit.

Religion used to raise people's minds to a world of light and freedom from dirt and toil, transforming their experience and thereby "saving their world." Now perhaps it needs to help us get back in touch with our bodies. We must transform our antiseptic urban culture and save our world by returning to our senses and the pleasure of being incarnate.

Sharing orgasm with another person can be powerful. It intermixes vibes and spiritual resonances, intermingling people's karma. For this reason sex carries major consequences; we should be circumspect about whom we have sex with (though, clearly, many gay venues do not allow for such circumspection). In a burgeoning relationship, mutual arousal and orgasm pump the hormones, neurotransmitters, and psychic energies that generate the experience of being in love. In a long-term relationship, this sharing synchronizes the partners' vibes to deepen and strengthen their bond. Even the

Catholic Church now acknowledges that, in addition to pro-creation, "conjugal bliss" and strengthening emotional bonds are legitimate purposes of sex.

It is joyful and healing for a couple to writhe together in the throes of pleasure, activating the flow of energies through their chakras and stimulating the production of serotonin and endorphin in their nervous systems. Orgasm manifests the joy of being alive. In mythological terms, pleasure is the way God enjoys creation. And God's enjoyment—his "Behold, it is good"—manifests in us as our experience of the pleasure of fleshly incarnation.

While sex doesn't have to be meditation or prayer, it can still be more than most of us make it. Sex—and especially masturbation ("soloving")—can be experienced as a practice of consciousness of God. Instead of thinking of sex as wicked and ungodly—as the religions often enjoin their flocks to do—we can experience sexual arousal as a journey of the soul into sacred mythic space. In this space the deep forces of life, embodiment, and autonomous hormonal instinct for pleasure take over and allow ego to dim. In this underworld—in the Greek mythological sense of a subconscious, transpersonal substrate—sexual arousal is truly worship. Indeed, in gay personal ad jargon, body worship is a style of sex. It is adoration, reverence, and love for the evolutionary forces that have created the world we live in and shaped us into human beings—incarnate consciousness.

It is easier to be aware of the presence of God during sex than at almost any other time (except, of course, during meditation and ritual, when that's the point). Most things in our daily experience—driving a car or baking a cake—require attention to the particulars of what we're doing. Sex isn't about particulars. When we understand sexual arousal as participation in the joy of life and celebrating incarnation, then it is always an experience of God, of the *élan vital*, loving life.

If you follow the Christian admonition to treat everyone

you meet as though he were Jesus, when you meet another gay man you can openly embrace his feelings, needs, insecurities, and human foibles. And when you see that he is a manifestation of Jesus Christ himself, you can make love with him and share your homosexuality together in joyful and satisfying affirmation of your mutual divinity.

Why wouldn't you want to give that—your most precious treasure: yourself as a sexual being—to Jesus? Wouldn't he, of all beings, deserve your best gift?

Sex as Giving

Certainly, gay men sometimes respond affirmatively to self-focused, selfish eroticism. Sometimes that's what's hot about anonymous sex: One person's single-minded focus on his own pleasure gives the other person permission to be similarly focused. The paradoxical selfishness generates more pleasure for both. But when you give pleasure to another person you usually get a higher return of pleasure yourself. Give it away and it comes back multiplied. This creates a challenge: To pursue an essentially self-serving desire, we have to transcend self, to experience our self intimately bound up with another person's self.

This may be especially challenging for straight people. Of course, many couples make wonderful, ego-transcending love together, but because males don't understand female pleasure, they are sometimes unsure how to pleasure their partners and so focus only on their own satisfaction. In fact, this sexual self-centeredness is sometimes valorized as macho. But it makes for unsatisfying sex. And it has resulted in the demonization of female pleasure and the inculcation of frigidity in generations of multiply oppressed women.

It is such a kindness to have sex with another man, to choose him, to give generously to another, who needs the affirmation of his own worth and sex appeal, just as we do.

In romantic, subject-to-subject self-pleasuring—the kind of intercourse with our partners most of us seek—the pleasuring is mutual and self-reinforcing. We feel in our own bodies what's happening in the body of our homosexual partner. We resonate.

Curious Bodies

The necessary corollary of affirming pleasure is that incarnation in the flesh is a thing to be honored, relished, and celebrated. Such an affirmation directly challenges the dualistic notion that the soul and body are separate, even conflicting, entities. Body and soul are not in opposition. The body is good.

It's a kindness to others to show your body and to enjoy seeing the bodies of others. Because our sexual awareness is tied into vision and objectification, we males especially long to see others' bodies. We feel frustrated when we can't satisfy our curiosity. For gay men, nudity is an affirmation of us as curious bodies. It feels good to go bare-chested. It's a delight to see other men with their shirts off. It reminds us we're in pleasure-loving flesh. Nudity is good.

People clothe themselves for decoration and for protection from the elements (and these days, unfiltered UV radiation). Clothes are wonderful. One of the joys of being gay is often knowing how to dress well: to adorn oneself and others in ways that create beauty and interest. People also clothe themselves for protection from other people's judgment and sexual interest. Clothing can enhance attractiveness by hiding flaws. (Though that kind of thinking supports the notion that there *are* such things as flaws.) The obsession with hiding our bodies causes untold suffering, unhappiness, and frustration. Baring all allows these anxieties to abate. Naked, we forget to be ashamed of our bodies.

In our all-male world, we seldom worry about being raped if we show our bodies. In the straight world this is a real concern. Women are raped in part because sexually repressed, angry males rebel against the competitive, hierarchical system designed to restrict sex to alpha males through the dynamic of women's selectivity. Rapists force themselves on women who are helpless or who they imagine to be "asking for it" by the women making themselves attractive. Modesty is both a mechanism of self-defense for women and a demonstration of power and ownership by dominant males. (Middle Eastern cultures that veil women and seclude them from public view demonstrate this in the extreme.)

In a very practical way, feeling good about one's body and showing it proudly—and appropriately, of course—helps self-esteem, allays neurosis and anxiety, and motivates one to take good care of oneself. Concern with the body is not foolish vanity; rather, it is good stewardship over one's place in creation. Taking care of yourself and sharing your success in that endeavor with others is a simple, practical way of creating beauty and improving a little piece of the world. Appropriate nudity is a dramatization and demonstration of God's primordial "Behold, it is good."

A Matter-of-Factness About Sexuality

Sex needn't be such a big deal. There is no reason it should be an occasion for shame. The obsession with rules about sex distorts and spoils many (maybe even most) people's experience of life. Neurosis and antisocial behavior result from craziness and frustration about sex.

While gay culture has certainly produced some pretty crazy manifestations of sex, there's a simple matter-of-factness about sexuality in our lives that is refreshing and liberating. In this, we're part of a larger phenomenon, maybe not even the biggest manifestation of it—though we tend to be blamed for it by the people who don't like the loosening of the old taboos.

The larger phenomenon, characterized as the sexual

revolution, is evidenced in the fact that sex is being valued for its own sake, not just a means to the biological end of reproduction. Masturbation, for example—privately, in groups, or with others over the Internet—is now acknowledged as a normal, even healthy behavior. This larger phenomenon is the transformation of morality away from taboos and rules about what's forbidden and toward cultivation of compassion and kindness as motivation for what's to be encouraged.

Sex reminds us to be in the present. Of course, a lot of the sexual fantasy that accompanies sex play is about the past, but the experience of pleasure is necessarily in the present. You don't really enjoy sex unless you're aware and present in your body, not caught up in the mind-stuff that distracts from the present. Orgasm itself stops the mind-stuff. There are no ideas in your head while you're coming—no content, just experience and consciousness.

Pornography as Good

Pornography is good. Well, maybe not *all* examples of pornography are good. Some porn flicks have terrible production values. Some depict bad attitudes and depersonalize people by showing them as victims or unwilling participants. Some porn, especially straight porn, champions polarization and male dominance. Some gay porn eroticizes negative behavior—a result of the unfortunate notion that since we're considered "sinners," we might as well demonstrate how sinful we can be, just to spite the righteous.

But in general, gay porn depicts willing, enthusiastic partners enjoying themselves and giving joy to others. In a sex-positive context, it's a generous thing for attractive men to share their zest for sexuality with others by allowing their sexual adventures to be photographed.

There are downsides, of course. Some consumers become

obsessed and "addicted" to porn. Some lose their ability to stir internal arousal because they become dependent on the external presentation of it. Sometimes porn causes problems between partners who have different degrees of interest in it: One partner may feel left out of the other's arousal pattern because it's focused on the fantasy instead of the reality of the two individuals together in love. Such problems are more likely to appear in straight relationships, where men and women have different responses to visual sexual stimuli. Homosexuals are more likely to be on the same wavelength and to share cognate fascination with other men's bodies.

In a way, porn is always inadequate and even disappointing. Mere images of a man's body can never show the drama of emotion and pleasure going on inside him. Even the most uninhibited and enthusiastic porn star can only faintly suggest what his sexual arousal feels like. That's because sexual arousal and pleasure have no content. They are dynamics of consciousness and can only be experienced, not conceptualized. The wild rush of sensation and excitement that comes from having sex just can't be captured on film. To get it, you must participate.

This is true of all experience. It's one of the secrets of life: Thinking about experience is not having the experience. The only way to live is to live. (Remember Agnes Gooch in *Auntie Mame*!)

Perhaps the biggest downside to porn is that it artificially and unrealistically raises the bar of attractiveness. Too many of us feel inadequate because we can never measure up to the hot men on the small screen. But the problem isn't that too many men are attractive, but that some of our egos are so damaged, we can't take joy in other people's lives without turning their good fortune around and making it an indictment of ourselves.

Whatever one thinks about pornography and erotica, there's clearly a difference between gay and straight examples of the genre. Gay porn tends to emphasize equality, spontaneity, and naturalness. (Part of the gay psychological struggle is to feel that gayness is natural.) Straight porn emphasizes the extremes: Women are heavily made up and display them- selves to look sexually available, and men have to be domi- nant and victorious. For straights, the polarity of male and female is what's most sexually exciting.

Straight society and mainstream religion have terribly jaundiced opinions of pornography. It's a shame they can't appreciate porn through the eyes of gay men. And it's a shame religion teaches straight people to resent other people's sexu- al joys. Porn provides a chance to live other people's life expe- riences. It allows you to imagine being in other bodies—a reminder of the mystical truth that the Being in you *is* also the Being, the consciousness, in others. While aroused in the pres- ent moment of pleasure, you feel your connection with other men. You enjoy their sexiness. You resonate with the "mysti- cal body" of all gay men.

With porn you get to be the invisible watcher; you share in others' sexual joys without your own ego getting in the way. You're in God's position, seeing with God's eyes—totally unin- volved—just observing and experiencing joy in the watching, not the doing. Porn, in fact, can be a wonderful opportunity to practice the virtuous attitude Buddhism calls "joy in the joy of others." Our joy comes from being pleased that the models had a great experience—an experience we'd have enjoyed hav- ing ourselves—and being pleased that they were generous and daring enough to allow us to share the experience with them through the technologies of photography and video.

Male Beauty

One of the remarkable things about gay consciousness is that we apply the male tendency to be sexually aroused by visual experience to other men. We appreciate male beauty.

Beauty is a quality often restricted to females: Women are

beautiful; men are handsome. Female beauty implies sexual availability and the power to influence and manipulate men. Handsomeness suggests a whole range of qualities well beyond mere sexual attractiveness. It implies authority and successfulness, the power to control other people, especially women. Beauty is an attribute of youth that fades with age. Handsomeness increases with age (because it demonstrates male prowess).

Male beauty differs significantly from female beauty in that it is more natural and less contrived. Male beauty is not modulated by makeup or the intentional alteration of the body to fit a socially determined model (from high heels, push-up bras, and girdles to breast implantation). While men might use bronzers and a little eye shadow to enhance their appearance, they employ these aesthetic tools with utmost subtlety. They might work out at a gym, but part of a man's beauty is that he needn't try to look beautiful; he just *is* beautiful. Societal ideals of female beauty are totally different. The beauty of a glamorous, adorned woman is an illusion created with makeup; she intentionally wears a mask.

Likewise, sexy male poses look different. Muscles are pumped, of course, and any "pose" is contrived. But the poses men assume usually look natural and candid. Women's sexy poses look intentionally exaggerated and artificial. The woman makes herself up and assumes an awkward posture—she presents herself—to suggest she is available for sex.

The movies have helped to establish the idea that men can be objects of sexual desire—in the eyes of women, at least. In show business we certainly find examples of breathtakingly attractive, sexy men. But for the most part, men in Western society do not have to be beautiful the way women must. Men don't have to take care of themselves. Women are supposed to overlook aesthetic considerations in favor of a man's bank account and prowess. In fact, straight males are not supposed to want to be beautiful, for appreciation of beauty is a male trait. A beautiful man risks being attractive to other men, which might threaten his straight identity. Straight men shouldn't want to appear attractive because that would make them like women: dependent on someone else's assessment of them. But of course they do, and are sometimes confused and conflicted by that.

Straight men, like gay men, go through a process of body questioning and body image development. They may have a harder time because their conditioning does not allow them to look at other men's bodies. How can they assess penis size, for instance, if they are ashamed to display their penises around other men at the gym and afraid to look at the penises that are on display? (They require the testimony of women, though they scorn women who've had enough experience to be competent witnesses.)

There's a developmental process all gay men go through. Because our sense of self is bound to our perception of other men's beauty, we ask ourselves how we compare with other men. Male beauty can be an ordeal. Gay men experience both the appreciation of beauty and the desire to be appreciated. This is one of the major sources of gay men's suffering— because self-esteem gets confused with sexual desirability.

The Problem of Looksism

The male propensity to judge and to construct hierarchies bedevils us gay men in the area of sexual attraction. Our desire to have sex with the most attractive men we can find ends up creating frustration for us. We tend to want sex with men more attractive than we are in order to bolster our sense of our own attractiveness. This results in the phenomenon known in gay political circles as looksism: bias toward people who are *very* sexually attractive and against those who are less so. Always looking up the hierarchy of beauty means you're never attractive enough yourself and that men who desire you must be less attractive or they wouldn't want you: You can never be satisfied. The self-help side of the gay political/cultural movement has always recognized looksism as a source of oppression but has never really offered a solution.

Spiritual wisdom tells us that the only answer to suffering is to acknowledge things as they are, to do what you can to change the things you *can* change and to accept the rest, dis-identifying yourself from your ego. Suffering is the occasion to seek higher consciousness, and it is a clue from the universe that there is more than this. Suffering is a sign that you are called to something higher and that you *can* escape your own ego and suffering by relaxing your hold on your own opinions and judgments. Suffering—including assaults on your self-esteem—is the call to wake up.

The physical reality that generates the problem of looksism is also the world in which there are breathtakingly beautiful men. When we are happy for them, we get to share their joy and we move our focus away from ourselves. The way to get over looksism is to forget about it—to live in the present moment and drop all the worries and judgments that reside in associations with the past. Then we can be at peace with ourselves and enjoy men's beauty without taking it personally and without resenting others by comparing ourselves to them. Indeed, we should want beautiful men to be as beautiful in soul and virtue as they are in body and visage, for the sake of all of us.

Beauty has no content. It is experience itself: a mode of consciousness awakening to the consensual world produced by the multiplicity of creative beings. The experience of beauty is a direct experience of being alive. The experience of beauty also contains a sense of sadness and poignancy, because beauty reminds us of death and transitoriness. In some ways, it is the ephemeral character of beauty that makes it beautiful.

The Romantic poets proposed: Beauty is truth, truth beauty. Of course, Keats was speaking about a Grecian urn, but the idea is valid nonetheless. For men, at least, the perception of beauty is a sign of truth. We are deeply moved by what we see as beautiful. Beauty has metaphysical implications. For many of us, the proof of our homosexual orientation is precisely the pang we feel when we see a beautiful man. That's the indisputable evidence of the truth of our identity.

Male beauty is my own beauty. What is beautiful in other men, I want to be beautiful in myself. Male beauty inspires awe at creation. And gay men are *remarkably* beautiful; gay men glow. Appreciation of that beauty is participation in the divine assessment of creation.

Drag

Gay men do sometimes put on makeup and display themselves in an exaggerated, artificial manner, not to look like men but to look like women. The straight world has often misunderstood this phenomenon—along with some homosexuals who didn't understand the joke—and thought it meant gay men really want to be women. (Of course, the phenomena of transsexuality and gender change are very real in some people's lives. And there are spiritual implications and karmic resonances that go with this, though, like lesbian spiritualities, they are beyond the purview of this book.) But gay men generally don't want to be women: What would we do without our penises?

Drag—and especially the genderfuck drag that has been championed by gay hippies and Radical Faeries—is about making light of traditional gender-role conventions. It's about allowing men to enjoy the variety and style in dress accorded to women. (Though real women could never be so fabulous.) Drag is about costume, not about sex.

Among some male prostitutes, cross-dressing is a ploy for getting customers, and among some of those customers it's a ploy for getting homosexual sex without appearing to know that's what's happening. It's part of keeping the closet shut for some straight-identified men. But for the most part, gay men don't dress up in drag to cruise for sex.

For many men, especially at Halloween, donning a dress and putting on makeup is a liberating, whimsical defiance of society's overarching concern that men's and women's roles and identities stay separate. Gay psychotherapy groups often make Halloween a time for a special kind of therapy session, complete with fashion show, just to loosen the screws and relax the margins of what's acceptable. Perhaps drag even releases deep psychological stresses.

Comedians, of course, have long made drag an element of humor—from Shakespeare to Milton Berle. All people, straight and gay, get a charge and a laugh from seeing these rules violated. Because of the ridiculousness of the comedians, the violation of gender roles doesn't seem like violation of sex roles. In fact, the playful acceptance of drag (exemplified in the cult popularity of *The Rocky Horror Picture Show*) is a sign the rigidity of straight society is loosening. Even straight men can dress up for Halloween. Drag is a sign—and a mechanism—of the transformation of culture and the relaxing of male dominance imperatives that gay liberation produces. It's also an important sign of our ability to comprise both masculinity and femininity and to transcend gender roles.

The Secret of Tiresias

Our homosexuality reveals something that most straight men have a hard time even thinking about. This is the secret of Tiresias.

Tiresias was the mythical Greek soothsayer who was changed from male to female, then after seven years back again. He was asked whether the man or the woman has the better experience of sex (that is, whether he preferred being the top or the bottom). Tiresias answered that the female has the better position in sex. It's more pleasurable to be receptive; bottom is better. This is something the straight male world desperately resists.

The gay world confounds these roles. Gay men are actually able to share the experience of Tiresias. We can be both top and bottom. We can actually be both top and bottom *at the same time*!

One of the most debilitating consequences of conventional gender-role conditioning is that males are taught to bring the issues of male dominance to the sex act. This results in an exaggerated concern for coitus and ejaculation. Male competition and scarcity anxieties cause men to fear they won't be able to maintain an erection long enough to complete "the act," so they abbreviate the sex to ensure penetration and ejaculation. Male preoccupation with hierarchy as well as right and wrong causes men to worry about performance and about the acceptability of pleasure itself. Certain kinds of stimulation (for example, anal touching or even nipple play) and certain kinds of feelings (vulnerability and affection) are considered wrong; they are too womanly or too queer. Foreplay is curtailed—even the name *foreplay* suggests that lovemaking and touching aren't actually part of sex. Thus men conditioned into straight roles—whether heterosexual or homosexual—limit their sexual arousal to their penises and disdain romance. (The manifestation of this dynamic in homosexual activity is the idea that one man must "conquer" the other and that the bottom's anal pleasure should be portrayed as painful.)

Sex Play

Our homosexuality tells us that sex play is a much richer experience than just fucking. Because there is no clear "purpose" to homosexual sex—no "natural goal," such as the insemination of the female—all of it is sex *play.*

According to the Catholic Church, any sex play that is not at least potentially open to the possibility of a sperm cell impregnating an ovum is mortally sinful and deserves eternal punishment. Only one kind of sex is allowed. For straight people, ejaculation must happen in the female vessel or it isn't "real sex." Straight-role indoctrination insists that sex be justified. Even when partners use contraceptives, the style of the act is supposed to be one that would allow the possibility of conception. Obviously, straight people, especially men, have sex for pleasure, but the indoctrination shames this. Masturbation is ridiculed and dismissed as an inadequate substitute for the real thing. (In the 1990s a U.S. Surgeon General was forced to resign for suggesting that masturbation could be promoted in sex education classes as a way to reduce teenage pregnancies.)

Straight role indoctrination also dismisses women's pleasure as irrelevant, even unseemly. A woman doesn't need an orgasm to get pregnant. And the way men are supposed to have sex is not particularly conducive to women's response. Of course, there are voices in society teaching something different: Masters and Johnson and Dr. Ruth Westheimer, for example. In marriage counseling, heterosexual couples are instructed to break with these often unspoken cultural rules and use their sexuality to enhance their emotional relationship, not just to perform. Thus husbands and wives may learn to pleasure each other in a variety of ways that don't include penetration. Even so, husbands are unlikely to share this with other men.

But for gay people, it really doesn't matter what triggers the orgasm. Certainly, most sex play aims at orgasm, and for men that means ejaculation, but a great variety of activities generate sexual arousal and bring on orgasm: oral, anal, intercrural, interfemoral, manual, frictional, simultaneous, sequential, from the front, from behind, on the belly, on the back, with toys or without. We don't have to be goal-oriented.

Gay sex is always about more than just fucking—because the roles aren't static, they have to be figured out through interpersonal dynamics. There is a negotiation that hetero-sexuals never experience that gay men go through to determine who's on top and who's on the bottom or whether they might alternate roles. Of course, this isn't true in a bathhouse or sex club, where participants leave their identities at the door, but it is true in dating or even tricking.

Besides, for gay men the appreciation of another man's beauty is more likely to make us want to touch him than just fuck him. Sexual prowess is experienced just in the penis, while the pang of beauty is felt throughout the body. This alters our vision of power in society. It helps us to be aware of the degree to which male behavior is motivated by the need to be on top—in a variety of senses.

Homosexual coitus in which one person penetrates the other is only one form of homosexual sex. Because we gay people are also inundated with the culture's indoctrinating messages, we too can get stuck on the impregnation model. The gay media, especially the sexually explicit side of the media, tends to reinforce the notion that the proper culmi-nation of sex play is fucking. For gay men this means anal fucking—the style of intercourse that most closely mimics heterosexual coitus. The messages around us establish the penis ejaculating inside another person as the apex of sex. But lesbians have great sex without any penises at all. Many gay men don't particularly care for anal intercourse, and these days awareness of sexually transmitted diseases and the need for condoms discourage penetrative intercourse. Though, of course, for many others it is indeed the natural apex of sex, a wonderful expression of intimacy, and a great source of pleasure (especially to the bottom).

Perhaps the least contrived style of sex play is frottage:

"belly fucking"—partners simply touch, hug, kiss, and squeeze each other until they both come. It requires the least preparation and least intention. There's no competition, though there is the drive to get closer together. Along with mutual masturbation, this may be one of the most common ways gay people make love—especially in long-term relationships where expression of sexual affection is a nightly event and so gets simplified to the easiest and most affectionate. It is also the safest, with the least potential for spreading contagion.

But anal fucking is what gets all the attention because it upsets conservative straight people the most. It's the only way they imagine gay sex, because vaginal fucking is the only way they imagine—or allow—straight sex. It violates cleanliness taboos, and gay men who enjoy anality learn to transform their experience of physicality and dirtiness, thereby liberating themselves from infantile conditioning about defecation. That liberation is psychologically beneficial—as is our liberation from the notion that penetration must be part of the sex act. Good sex is about affection and pleasure, not performance.

Fidelity and Longevity

Sexual fidelity is not the linchpin of relationship. Of course, a period of exclusivity is usually part of a new romance and often the foundation of a long-lasting and trusting relationship. But as the relationship matures, gay men have discovered, a certain amount of independent or shared recreational sex play can in fact strengthen the bonds by allaying fears of being trapped or "fenced in."

Within limits, the gay world offers occasions for recreational sex play that are anonymous and impersonal enough not to threaten stable, committed relationships. Going to the baths or a JO club together, for instance, can be a way for a gay couple to spice up their sex life a little—perhaps while they're on vacation in a strange city—without threatening the partners' commitment to one another. (Of course, hygiene concerns must be respected.)

The gay freedom to expand the sexual possibilities of a loving relationship, and to experiment with different styles of fidelity and play, distresses conservative forces. Pro-family advocates say gay marriage threatens straight marriage precisely because gay people might find ways of doing it better—of being happier and more fulfilled. The straight male concern with hierarchy and competition demands we not even be allowed to try to do it if there is a chance we'll do it better. It must really gall them that Masters and Johnson found that gay men have *better* sex!

Certainly, the common notion in straight culture that infidelity demands divorce has it all backwards. Supposedly in the interest of preserving families, the gender-role conventions establish a draconian penalty: A single failure spells the termination of the relationship. If "family values" means providing a stable nest in which to rear children, why would exclusivity concerns hold the family hostage? This all-or-nothing requirement doesn't recognize differences in partners' needs at different times in their lives and doesn't honor the relationship except as a pact that allows each partner to claim possession of the other's sexuality. Besides, sexual exclusivity is based on concern for the preservation of genetic lineage, not the dynamics of love and trust.

You wonder why straight people don't have something like JO clubs. Of course, the answer is obvious: Men and women have different sexual response patterns, women are less likely to seek that kind of anonymous play, and without women, men can't allow themselves to be sexually aroused. Traditionally, houses of prostitution have served as sex clubs for men. But at every level these are disparaged, even oppressed by the police. Besides, a straight couple can't very well go to a house of prostitution together. Still, straight people ought to be able to celebrate and play with sexuality in positive and socially approved venues (perhaps created under the auspices of churches—to show that mainstream religion can be sex-positive!).

This is something they could learn from the gay world. The sexual liberation of women and the general relaxing of anxieties about homosexuality and bisexuality, combined with new technologies (like virtual reality), may make such opportunities possible. Relieving sexual stress on straight men would reduce the general ambiance of violence in modern urban society and probably result in less crime, especially crimes of sexual violence.

Longevity also is not the linchpin of a relationship. Many gay men do not achieve this, though far more do than the cultural stereotypes allow. And almost all of us have gone through a phase of adventuresome promiscuity. Gay men are likely to be wanderers—a sign of our freedom from traditional expectations. We've likely had a variety of relationships: This doesn't represent failure, just a different style of life. In fact, for most of us, it's clearly a kind of success.

The gay experience for men includes a lot of sex. Our gay perspective shows us that the mainstream model of one monogamous partner for life is a consequence of the obligations of parenthood. Without the need to balance priorities and parental obligations, the imperatives for that kind of relationship change.

Since God's love for creation is manifested as your partner's love for you and your love for your partner, a satisfying, stable relationship—full of sexuality, affection, and romance—is a blessing to be cultivated, especially as one gets older and the sexual intensities of youth cool. To find happiness one must create a life rich in friends, associates, and loved ones, but that life doesn't have to look like the traditional heterosexual family. It should include sexual experience and adventure. Longevity isn't an obligation or a commandment, but it might be a prize that comes with the adventure.

Altered States of Consciousness

Some gay people use drugs to enhance the pleasure of sex. The various altered states of consciousness produced by drugs generally give pleasure directly, though it is different from sex—not experienced in the body as much as in consciousness itself. This is not to argue that drug use always results in better sex—for some people the opposite is true—but that many of the objections to drug use sometimes exacerbate the problems they claim to address because they are the products of negative, judgmental attitudes toward pleasure.

Drugs reveal interesting things. Alteration of mental states provides a higher-order experience of *being conscious*. That the nature of consciousness is easily changed by the ingestion of an herb or chemical imparts awareness of the arbitrariness of the content of consciousness. Most of our ordinary consciousness is focused entirely on the content, but in the altered state you notice the vessel that holds the content. Of course, sex itself is an altered state of consciousness—one that calls us to be aware of our bodies, and our selves, in new and different ways. It too calls us beyond the usual content.

Gay people generally use drugs to engage in adventure and to enhance sex and pleasure, not to suppress pain. Conservative society presumes that it is emotional problems and unhappiness that motivate drug use. This is an error that dramatically affects public policy. Certainly, many people do self-medicate emotional pain with drugs and alcohol. Certainly, drug and alcohol use can spiral into unhappiness caused by drug dependence and addiction, and unhappy, sexually conflicted homosexuals, especially, face these dangers because drugs and alcohol temporarily relieve the conflicts.

Nonetheless, the main reason people use drugs is to expand consciousness and enhance experience. And the main reason gay men use drugs is to enhance sex.

As Randy Conner shows in *Blossom of Bone,* gay men and lesbians who use drugs resonate with a long tradition—reaching far back into hunter-gatherer times—of sexually variant individuals experimenting with techniques for inducing ecstatic states and alteration of consciousness for mystical purposes. These individuals were the medicine men, shamans, and wise old crones who anchored the spiritual lives of their tribe and entered these altered states for the good of the collective as well as for their own personal experience of transcendence.

They also experimented on themselves to learn the effects of the various mushrooms, berries, cactuses, and leaves that nature offered. Some people surely died in the process of discovering that certain plants were not edible. Because they were outside the reproductive structure of the tribe, they could risk this possibility. Parents with children couldn't jeopardize their lives just to see what a newly noticed mushroom might do to them if they ate it. That responsibility was reserved to the priests.

Today, because of the intensity of the biotech preparations of these mind-altering substances, drugs have taken on new significance. All sort of people use drugs when they shouldn't. And because we've lost our appreciation of the social role of non-reproducing people, people who could or should use drugs (for medical purposes, for instance) aren't allowed to.

Alcohol and tobacco companies use their political influence to keep their harmful drugs legal, while other benign, possibly beneficial drugs are outlawed. The legal system compounds the problem by its inability, or unwillingness, to distinguish beneficial drugs from harmful ones. Conservative society specifically forbids this kind of information. Marijuana, for instance, is obviously far less deleterious than alcohol, doesn't impair motor skills like alcohol, and generally makes recreational users friendly and peaceful rather than obstreperous and belligerent. Gay experience with bar life certainly shows us that alcohol can ruin lives. People aren't taught how to use drugs correctly. No one knows the real harms or real benefits.

Nobody pays attention to the findings of the self-experimenters. If you want to know about drugs, ask gay men who've experienced drug states—not Baptist preachers, politicians, or uptight ex-Army officers. This question brings us back to the observation in the introduction: that at stake in the current cultural transformation—of which gay liberation is a part—is whether truth is found in declarations by official authorities or in personal experience.

The power of drugs to transform consciousness can't be realized if consciousness hasn't formed properly in the first place. Society rightly tries to prevent children from altering their brain chemistry before their brains are fully formed. And parents rightly try to protect their children from engaging in grown-up delights before they are grown up.

Sex and drugs are problems for *parents*. The legal system treats everybody as though we are all parents and responsible for the upbringing of society's children, and in the process diminishes the responsibilities of the people who actually have children. Parents rightly try to draw out their children's maturation. Childhood is a wonderful time of freedom from adult concerns. The long childhood of human beings helped us evolve consciousness and intelligence. But parents are embarrassed by talk of pleasure, sex, and drugs; this kind of discussion is uncomfortable to have with children, too close to the incest taboo. So parents fail to fulfill their responsibilities for their children's upbringing and hope the legal system will do it for them by its treating everybody as though we are all children.

This creates a quagmire for us. Because, as gay people, we *are* outlaws, we are skeptical of many of the rules society imposes. We properly understand that some of these rules are important for parents to follow for the sake of their children's maturation, but they are not applicable to us. But we may also allow ourselves to bend these rules too far and thereby get ourselves in trouble. Mind-altering drugs are potent. It's important to use them properly and to know which ones to stay away from entirely.

From our gay perspective, we see that modern society handles these issues poorly, that many laws do more harm than good, that resisting only causes problems to persist. This perspective can also make us naive about the dangers of sex and drugs. Some of the drugs our gay culture permits (like crystal meth) can be terribly harmful. Some of the sexual behaviors we allow in the name of freedom and sexual rebellion can also be potentially unwholesome and dangerous. Just because something is forbidden by straight society doesn't necessarily make it desirable and beneficial for us!

But forbidding things doesn't stop people from indulging in them. The issue is less which particular drugs should be forbidden than whether prohibition is an effective way to deal with any drugs. (Prohibition certainly doesn't work to prevent homosexuality and maybe just demonstrates the principle "What you resist persists.") The greater problem is the dualistic thinking that makes some things forbidden and others not. Dualistic judgment—especially instead of conscious awareness, personal experience, and information—is the problem.

The Carrot Is Better Than the Stick

A gay stance, outside the impulses of male dominance, allows us to recognize one of the major discoveries of modern psychology: Threatening punishment is not the way to discourage unwanted behavior. Rewarding desired behavior works better. In fact, punishing undesired behavior results in an increase in the undesired behavior. Male aggressiveness cannot accommodate this discovery of behavioral science. But it's very important. It tells us how a psychologically aware society ought to deal with problems. And it demonstrates that violence does not solve problems. Nonviolence—merging masculine and feminine perspectives to achieve solutions—is a better way.

In fact, the failure of inspired literature like the Bible to reveal this simple truth is proof it is not "the instruction book for life" the evangelists proclaim it to be. Just as the Bible is wrong about the structure of the solar system, it is wrong about the threat of punishment and hellfire as an effective deterrent to unwanted behavior.

It may not be an automatically gay thing to see that punishment doesn't solve the problems it is supposed to, but it may be easier for us to conceive of changing things because we have so little stake in the status quo. More specifically, we're often excluded and threatened by society's system of punishment, which may be used arbitrarily against us. Our perspective enables us to reconceive of how society should shape its members' behaviors.

Rehabilitation

At the beginning of the 21st century, America, "Land of the Free," has the largest population of prisoners in the history of the world. Something needs to change. The penal system makes more criminals, not fewer, because it teaches violence. It vulgarizes society and puts out bad vibes. You have only to visit somebody in jail to be abused and mistreated yourself. Our current system raises the level of anger and rage in the society. And it destroys the moral and spiritual lives of the guards and prison officials as surely as it embitters the lives of the prisoners.

This dismal situation is the product of straight male domination values. Since straight men cannot speak out without compromising their masculinity, perhaps we gay men must remind society of the important wisdom: Reward changes behavior. The alleviation of security anxieties and the sense of being loved heal neuroses. The frustration of sexual desire produces violence. The fulfillment of the longing for touch and arousal makes for harmony. Love saves the world.

There's a link between homosexuality and prison life. Inevitably a kind of homosexuality flourishes in penal systems. In the absence of women, straight men exert their sexual dominance over other men. Men in prison have homosexual sex even when they're not gay in our modern psychological and political senses. And prison sex is fetishized by gay men—it's often portrayed in porn videos and allotted props in bathhouses and sex clubs. Moreover, legislators are loath to repeal antiquated sodomy laws, and gay men are still sometimes imprisoned simply for being gay.

Gay intuition tells us that a lot of the violence in society comes from people not feeling loved and appreciated. Don't you sometimes think that some of these crazy men who commit atrocious acts really just needed to be hugged? When you see young thugs, don't you sometimes think what they really want is to be held and comforted, that all their unattractive straight male bravado and posturing is just a cover for the need to feel loved by another man—an equal, a friend? Doesn't it sometimes seem that homosexuality might be the cure for all the problems of straight men?

Prison might more effectively rehabilitate unsocialized people if it were a cross between the Body Electric and an enlightenment training or 12-step program. 12-steppers care about each other; they readily ask one another for help and support. The enlightenment training of the Human Potential Movement teaches that everybody is God and that, by agreement, everybody should take turns treating one another that way. When you arrive at such a seminar, "greeters" wait at the door to tell you how magnificent you look and to assist you to your seat. After all, you are God and deserve to be treated respectfully.

That's not how prison guards treat their prisoners. Instead of helping prisoners feel magnificent, they belittle, abuse, and terrorize them, making them feel worthless and criminal. They reinforce the very self-fulfilling prophecies rehabilitation is supposed to change.

Wouldn't nondominant, non–goal-oriented sexual arousal do more to transform prisoners' difficult lives? Wouldn't they do better to learn to erotically stimulate one another instead of to abuse one another? What if instead of being brutalized and treated like animals, prisoners were treated like special guests? Suppose they spent 12 hours a day enraptured as their brother prisoners caressed and massaged their bodies into a state of mystical sexual arousal. Suppose that every afternoon they reached a "big draw" and experienced their oneness with God and their brother and sister human beings. Maybe they wouldn't have to be locked up for 30 years; they'd be rehabilitated in a few weeks. The problem would be getting them to leave.

Of course, the time to rehabilitate these men is before they got to prison, before they committed any crimes. Those lessons in oneness with God and other people need to be taught before violence arises in their lives. Of course, anger and rebelliousness have deep roots in economic oppression and inequality; those issues have to be addressed. Teenagers jacking off won't solve crime and violence. But their learning to do so in positive, self-affirming, spiritually informed ways might make a great difference. Relaxing the stress from sex- and gender-role rules might help alleviate some of the violence, and gentle society in general. Perhaps schools and churches ought to be teaching the Body Electric work. Perhaps priests and ministers should all be trained in erotic spirituality.

This is fanciful speculation. It's also an interesting example of how our gay experience allows us to look at the world differently and to see the fallacies other people take for unquestionable truth.

The morality that Western religion teaches is exactly

backward. Just as the laws of Prohibition exacerbated most of the problems they were said to address, morality based on guilt and the threat of divine punishment serves to increase the incidence of undesired behavior. Living in fear of divine punishment presumes a neurotic personal God who imposes arbitrary rules, especially about sex and pleasure. The biblical God calls Himself a jealous God—jealous when humans pay attention to other representations of divinity. He is also jealous of fleshly pleasure that does not increase the number of His believers. Morality based on punishment is rife with conflict: between God and humanity and between competing groups of human beings.

A better basis for morality is the belief that the personalities behind conflict—personality in God and personality in us—are just passing, superficial appearances of consciousness. Out of compassion for all other expressions of consciousness, we're naturally moved to live cooperatively and harmoniously, to ease one another's suffering. The "reward" for living that kind of life *is* living that kind of life. True morality—integrity, compassion, and kindness—is its own reward.

These ideas about terrorism, male beauty, sexual morality, relationship styles, drugs, violence, punishment, and prison rehabilitation are just the author's speculation. Their content doesn't represent an "orthodoxy" of gayness. In fact, their content really isn't the point. The point is that they run counter to the prevailing social ethos because they derive from a perspective outside and challenging to the status quo. That doesn't necessarily make these ideas right, but considering what a mess the status quo has produced, perhaps some status quo–threatening ideas are worth entertaining. Introducing them demonstrates the gay role of religious teacher and spiritual guide.

Chapter 5
Things Our Homosexuality Tells Us About Religion

The natural tendency of so many gay people to be good and "religious" clashes with the religions' traditional rejection of homosexuality. Proof of this tendency is found in you, dear reader—in the fact that you are reading this book. You would not have selected it otherwise. If you were the debauched, dissolute pervert that popular religion accuses you of being, you wouldn't care what the religions say or seek to find meaning in your life. But you do. And this forces you to take a perspective on religion, to "twist" how you see all things religious and to move up a step into "spirituality." It demonstrates—to us, at least—that the guardians of religious orthodoxies don't really know what they're talking about.

Religious conservatives—especially those active in Christianity and Islam—want to go back to the old days when they imagine everything was idyllic and people behaved themselves out of appropriate fear of God. But the truth is, you can never go back; time can't be undone. Short of bombing the whole planet back to cave days, there is nothing that will make people believe in the old superstitions once they've seen beyond them. Preachers often proclaim that the cosmology of their religious doctrines is hard to believe in and therefore requires "faith." This is a sign there's something wrong with their cosmology. It simply doesn't fit experience. If you have to talk yourself into believing something "on faith," it isn't likely to guide your life.

Conservatives are also incorrect that things were better in

the past. The same problems existed: teenage pregnancy, rape, illegitimacy, venereal disease, and drunkenness. They just weren't discussed or acknowledged with the openness of today. Those same conservatives complain about "liberal bias" in the modern media because it *does* talk about these issues, as though hiding them would make them go away (gay life is an example). Besides, their old-time religion *was* responsible for true horrors: the Crusades, the Inquisition, the persecutions of so-called witches, the Nazi Holocaust and Russian pogroms, even the terrorism of the late 20th century and the early 21st.

Because modern gay people see that our homosexual predecessors were often the victims of religious atrocities, we are especially motivated to seek transformation. And our gay perspective shows us—and, if it would pay attention, the rest of the human race—how to proceed with the transformation. Indeed, we are part of the transformation, whether we realize it or not.

Gay people are intimately involved in this transformation because traditional religion has been so obsessed with condemning us and because our status as outsiders forces us to look at religion from a higher perspective, a more modern perspective. And this changes everything.

The wondrous, galactic-size universe discovered by science beggars the naive little man-size world of the ancients, where the religious traditions developed. Many of the issues facing modern humankind are not even addressed in the old mythologies: nuclear war, air travel, modern medicine (including cloning and DNA manipulation), television, telephone, drugs, and automobiles. All these have religious significance, but how to apply the old myths to new problems is perplexing. This is especially true of a new kind of human consciousness: modern homosexuality. The existence of consciously identified gay men and lesbians who understand their experience and claim a place in human ecology is a very new thing. And it has major relevance for debates about the other issues confronting the religions because, in a very positive and helpful way, it challenges the very nature of religion itself.

Joseph Campbell said we are living in the "terminal moraine of mythology." A moraine is the field of shattered rocks and debris ground down, pushed ahead, and finally deposited by a glacier; all the pieces of stone are broken and intermixed. So it is with the myths and religious doctrines that have come down to us from the past. Uprooted from their originating cultures and historical situations and syncretized with stories and symbols from other cultures, they've ended up a hodgepodge.

Today, this moraine has become "terminal"—that is, the glacier has reached the end of its path and the ice itself has melted away. Science has completely altered the world in which the myths arose. In the last 50 years humankind's vision has expanded out countless light-years to discover a cosmos so vast that every god humans have ever imagined pales in comparison. Before now, no one had any inkling of what was out there beyond the sky. It is truly in our day that the universe has been discovered.

What we've learned about the expanse of the heavens and the minuteness of the molecules and atoms (born in the deaths of ancient stars) far exceeds the explanations offered by primitive myths. Our religious practices and our spiritual aspirations must make sense in the context of this modern universe—if only because it is unequivocally true.

We are exposed to a dazzling array of ideas, including astronomy, psychology, evolutionary biology, ecology, Buddhist and Hindu meditation practice, yoga, the Gaia hypothesis, artificial intelligence speculation, and paranormal phenomena as well as traditional religion. Indeed, we are probably exposed to more information by age 7 than was known by all the great philosophers of the past put together.

From this barrage of information we have to *creatively* make sense of life—and of God.

We modern human beings must literally create our own religions; we have to figure out what makes sense to us and interpret sacred stories in ways consistent with the modern, global, scientifically modulated worldview. That worldview promises to keep changing faster than anybody can keep up with. It's a little scary. But it's also an opportunity.

Religion Shouldn't Be About Sex

The most obvious thing our gay perspective tells us about the nature of religion is that it shouldn't be about sex. That's not to say that the things religion *are* properly concerned with don't affect sex and sexual behavior, but that religion is about something much more important than preserving the sexual rules and gender-role conditioning of male-dominated society.

Religion should be about celebrating life, not circumscribing it. You don't need religion to tell you not to kill or steal—*the* two key issues of morality. They're self-evident. You need religious vision to motivate you to be loving, gentle, compassionate, and unafraid in the face of adversity. Historically, religion has been primarily about why we experience suffering, not about sex. Joseph Campbell hypothesized that the origins of religion lie in protohumans' sense of guilt at killing animals for food. Other theorists hypothesize that religion began with funeral rites and tales of afterlife to assuage grieving.

Once protohumans had developed enough sense of self to realize they didn't want to be killed and eaten themselves, they felt guilty about doing so to other living beings. Tribal shamans sought to communicate with those animal spirits, often with the help of herbs and plants that produced altered states of consciousness, to reconcile the animals' desire to live with humans' need to eat—and in the process, perhaps, discovered a transcendent world invisible to the ordinary senses. They told stories and created myths to explain, dramatize, and communicate what they'd experienced in their mystic reveries. Those stories gave meaning to the harsh realities of killing and dying. This was the beginning of religion. And this was the beginning of compassion, the true religious motivation.

Religious Founders

The characters we revere today as saviors—Jesus and the Buddha, for example—explained human suffering at a higher level of abstraction. The Buddha—Siddhartha Gautama, a nobleman turned beggar and spiritual seeker who lived in northern India in the fifth century before the Common Era—taught that the cause of suffering is frustration of desire and ignorance of what is truly desirable. He dismissed the elaborate system of gods and powers of Hindu religion as symbols for human ideas about the important issues of life, and preached that nobody can save you but yourself: You're on your own.

Buddha declared that a life of moderation and simplicity, guided by principles contained in the Eightfold Path (right belief, right intention, right speech, right action, right livelihood, right endeavoring, right mindfulness, right concentration) could bring an end to desire and frustration. Followers later summarized the moral teaching in what they called the Four Immeasurables: compassion, loving kindness, joy in the joy of others, and equanimity. Buddhists believe that holding these attitudes in mind will result in a life of less suffering for oneself and others. Moreover, such a way of life will free one from the karma that keeps repeatedly causing rebirth into the world of suffering.

Jesus Christ—the carpenter turned holy man in first-century, Roman-occupied Israel—taught that the cause of human suffering is "man's inhumanity to man" and that the answer is simple love of neighbor. He dismissed the elaborate system of ritual cleanliness and racial identity in Hebrew religion that prescribed strict obedience to the Law of the Torah, and said God should be considered a loving parent, not a demanding tyrant who had to be obeyed unquestioningly and appeased with blood sacrifices.

Jesus declared that life should be lived according to the Golden Rule: Do unto others as you would have others do unto you. Love of God and love of neighbor, including political enemies like the Romans, bring an end to cruelty and suffering. Christians believe that seeing Jesus in his followers and treating all people as though they were Jesus will produce a life of goodness and harmony and win one an eternal reward in heaven after death.

In the Beatitudes, Jesus too taught an "Eightfold Path" that turned the patriarchal, straight male values upside down: Be poor in spirit, mourn life's sorrows (don't avenge), be gentle, be hungry for righteousness, be merciful, be pure in heart, make peace, and accept persecution. When he was crucified, Jesus did not come down from the cross—something which the myth says he could have done—and smite the Romans and the temple priests. He did not respond according to the principles of male domination. "Getting even"—justice—is a notion born of dualistic beliefs in scarcity and in good and evil. Jesus showed how to respond to violence without vengeance.

As he let go of judgment and attachment to self, Gautama became conscious of a greater Self and saw the chain of causation leading from desire to suffering. This is configured mythologically as his recollection of his previous incarnations and his realization of the nature of karma. The so-called Law of Karma is the inverse of the Golden Rule: Others do unto you as you have done unto others. Expressed less magically, the modern-day maxim is: What goes around comes around.

Jesus' great mystical realization—his enlightenment—

was that the life in him was the same life that is in other people ("What you do to the least of these, you do to me"). This is the same life that is in nature and that provides the food we eat ("Unless you eat my body, you do not have life in you"), and the same life that is in God ("I and the Father are One").

Of course, everything in the cosmos is an incarnation of that life, but most people think of themselves as separate, vulnerable egos, polarized against the outside world. They don't realize their oneness with everything around them. Jesus' commandment was to love life, to see that same life in your neighbor, and for the sake of that life, to love your neighbor as yourself—not *as much as* (quantity) but *as* (identity): Your neighbor is yourself. Jesus' ministry demonstrated that if one is loving and sensitive to other people's needs, one transforms their lives, heals their pain, and ends their suffering. Jesus' miracles were manifestations of love of neighbor—and evidence of the power of good vibes.

Neither Buddha nor Jesus was especially concerned about supernatural things, but in the years after their deaths their followers mythologized their lives and declared them gods. The followers devised all sorts of otherworldly notions of afterlife and supernatural reality as metaphors for the founders' good advice about ending suffering and finding mystical oneness with all life.

Also, neither Buddha nor Jesus was particularly concerned about sex; neither taught sexual rules. The traditions that came to revere them, on the other hand, developed rules about sex based on metaphysical and theological teachings that were really just expressions of their culture's sex role and gender conventions.

To be fair, there are other great religious founders: Mahavira, Lao-tzu, Mohammed, Abraham, Kukulcán, Confucius, Wovoka, Ras Tafari, Bahá'u'lláh, Zoroaster, Manes, Bodhidharma, Nagarjuna, Martin Luther, Joseph

Smith, and Ramakrishna—some more historical or more famous than others. We shouldn't ignore them or dismiss their influence on history, but generally their religions were more tribal and local, and less influential, ultimately, than the religions of Jesus and Gautama (though Mohammed ended up with the greatest number of followers). They all developed spiritual systems to explain human experience and to help people live harmoniously. And of course, all the systems include rules about sex. But none of the religious founders ever emerged specifically to give sexual rules. None of them ever came with the message that sexual pleasure is the cause of all evil and that people who experience sexual pleasure deserve to be tortured mercilessly. Yet that's what religion has generally evolved into.

When you look at modern American religion, it seems like sex is the major concern—and condemning homosexuality the major imperative. Obviously, priorities are now turned upside down. The way we behave sexually ought to follow from the virtues religion teaches us, from the meaningful and inspiring messages it conveys about the reason for our existence. Religion's obsession with sex and threats of punishment is a sign it has lost the ability to move people through the power of its metaphors and spiritual teachings.

Religion should produce peace, harmony, and love; if it doesn't, something is wrong with it. When we look at the world, we see hatred, war, and inhumanity—mostly, consequences of religious differences. That's the evidence that religion needs transformation.

The old symbols, stories, and mythological explanations do not move people to feel compassion, to resonate with the universal life force, to feel love for our common environment, and to put the future of the human race ahead of their personal priorities for themselves and their own families.

Our gay sensitivity tells us that antisex, male-dominant gender-role conditioning ruins religion. Religion should teach people how to enjoy pleasure as wonderfully, profoundly, generously, and mystically as possible. Instead, it often scares them into neurosis. A modern, psychologically sophisticated religiousness has to impart positive messages about sex—and of course, homosexuality—that don't reinforce male-dominant gender conditioning and encourage mindless population growth. If we gay men and lesbians are participants in the founding of a new religious consciousness for humankind, Walt Whitman and Harry Hay belong in that list of great religious founders.

The Myths Don't Make Sense

If you're a Christian, you might feel saved by your personal relationship with God, exemplified in Jesus Christ. Still, the fundamental doctrine of salvation in Christianity—based on the mythology of bloody human sacrifice as fitting appeasement of God's wrath—probably doesn't speak to you. Your relationship with God and Jesus is likely something more loving and comforting—not the model of God as a stern, stiff-necked, patriarchal potentate demanding tribute. To you as a modern person, living in a liberal democracy, God as ruler of the universe is likely to more closely resemble a democratic leader administering government for the good of the governed than a dictator ruling for his own arbitrary pleasure.

What if we learned that in a small country in Africa or the Middle East a king has announced he's so offended by an act committed against his dynasty by a peasant 4,004 years ago that he has been considering burning alive all the inhabitants of his country? But he has decided that his rage can be assuaged instead just by the public torture and murder of his own first-born son. Wouldn't the free world be morally obligated to intervene? Wouldn't the United Nations have something to say? Wouldn't the United States send an envoy to talk some sense into this king?

This is essentially the story of God and Jesus as savior. That it sounds so ridiculous and repugnant is evidence that we've become more civilized than God, or at least more civilized than the people who thought up the stories about God. Though there is still a cult of Jesus' blood, most of that brutal thinking is dismissed by modern Christians. They are, naturally, transforming the myth in order to redeem it.

The model of the universe that Christianity perpetuates doesn't usefully serve modern humankind. It doesn't square with the physical cosmos that scientific observation reveals. The patriarchal model of God projects imperial government into the cosmos. Human beings are subjects cowed into obedience and fealty by threats of retaliation for minor offenses and lapses in cleanliness.

According to Christian doctrine, God is forever separate from His creation. Matter and spirit, creation and Creator, soul and body are eternally divided—even at odds—in a fiercely dualistic universe. This separation does not emerge from the religious, mystical basis of Christianity. Jesus didn't teach this. It is the fabrication of church officials and theologians eager to maintain the political and social status quo and to preserve the male domination of Western culture.

The theological argument for God as an omniscient judge turns religion into internalized policing. Even the mystical and social teachings of Jesus become another kind of threat. You're supposed to love your neighbor as yourself and see Jesus in everyone you meet, because if you don't God will damn you to hell. That is not what Jesus' commandment of love meant. The love that will save the world is the mystical vision of our common oneness.

More than a few mystics have been deemed heretics and threatened with death for reporting their mystical vision of oneness with God. You're not supposed to realize that *you* are God and that all the stories are about *you* and how *you* should experience life. But that's the correct way to understand it all.

Incarnation of God

Mythological statements that a particular guru or political/cultural hero is an incarnation of God are common all over the world. The numerous gurus from India who have become famous in America are frequently said to be incarnations of God. Haile Selassie, the emperor of Ethiopia during the Second World War, is recognized as God by the followers of Rastafarianism. In Christianity this particular appellation is reserved to Jesus Christ alone, but it is no different from other declarations of divine incarnation in other religions. Seeing that divinity is a common metaphor to apply to a spiritual teacher tells us that the point of such a metaphor is not to posit a metaphysical statement about the nature of that person but to proclaim the importance of the person's work and message.

The doctrine that Jesus is God is not a statement about Jesus. He himself would not have understood the idea that he was God, the Second Person of the Blessed Trinity. These are ideas born out of Greek philosophizing, not the ritual religion of the Hebrews. Jesus might actually have believed his life fulfilled the prophecy of a messiah who'd save his people from slavery and suffering, but he was more interested in teaching his message of interpersonal love than in establishing an honored place for himself in the pantheon of divine figures.

It still makes sense for us today to speak of the excellence of the commandment to love one another, to attribute this idea to Jesus of Nazareth, and to honor the idea by praising the man who articulated it. But the elaborate theological debates of early Christianity—about how Jesus could be both God and man at the same time, for example—missed the meaning of the metaphor. That particular debate resulted in animosity between Rome and Constantinople that continues even to the present. In fact, by bringing about the Great Schism and the centuries of enmity between the churches of the West and the East, the theologians demonstrated they hadn't understood Jesus' central teaching. When multitudes of human beings are massacred in battle to proclaim the message "Love your enemy," you can be sure the message hasn't been heard correctly.

The idea that Jesus was God—that is, that God became a human being—represents a profound development in the planetary soul of Earth. The One Mind of which we are all a part "realized" that divinity does not lie in an external God but within human consciousness. Jesus said God isn't outside you; rather, "the Kingdom of God is within you." This is the real meaning of the Incarnation.

It's a matter of perspective. Rise higher and the apparent dualities—between human and divine and also between all the other polarities that seem in conflict—turn out to be aspects of one another, just opposite sides of the same coin. That's actually the meaning of the statement "Jesus is God." It is not about the specialness of Jesus of Nazareth; it's about the divine aspects of human consciousness. The point of saying Jesus is God is to reveal that the rift between the human and the divine is an illusion.

This is also the meaning of Jesus' declaration "Love your enemies": Rise above difference and you'll see you're really one with those you'd thought of as enemies. You can't, of course, love your enemies. When you love them, they cease to be enemies. Jesus is the symbol—the code—for the deepest self in each of us. Jesus is not an external personage in the sky or some cosmic pal who gives us what we beg for. Jesus is the icon for our identity as sense organs for the planetary consciousness. Jesus is us, we are Jesus.

Of course, this insight into the nature of Jesus' role in

history isn't a uniquely gay insight. (Though it's not news to us that Christianity doesn't understand its own message.) But our gay perspective—our liberation from conventional thinking and from unquestioning acceptance of authority—allows us to understand the real meaning.

We honor Jesus by insisting that society be fair and loving, not by deifying him and murdering those who don't agree. We honor Jesus by recognizing his life as an event in history that embodied the human struggle to live a good life. We also honor Jesus when we work to end suffering—in our lives and in the lives of our loved one and neighbors. We don't honor him by saying, "Lord, Lord."

Faith

Not all gay people are spiritual giants—not even most—though the reverse might be true. If the spiritual giants of the past were alive today, almost all might recognize themselves as gay. This is certainly true of Native American two-spirit shamans and medicine people. It might be true of Jesus and Buddha. Who knows?

Your homosexuality can be a nudge in the direction of spiritual maturity: a challenge to be met, a transformation to undergo. There's no guarantee of success, of course, and lots of risk. In truth, the challenge life has thrown you is more a *gift* than a challenge. Your homosexuality is your faith.

Too often, faith for straight people means fitting in: giving up personal perspective to accept dogma and tradition—sometimes regardless of its incomprehensibility. For them, faith is faith in religion. Faith for gay people means the trust that our perspective from the social margins allows us to see a higher truth from a better angle. For straight people, faith is surrender. For gay people, faith is commitment and courage. Faith should mean trust in life, trust in the cosmic process.

Because we are told that if we are open and truthful about our sexual experience we cannot be inside, our homosexuality forces us to observe religion from outside. (This is true even of those in so-called affirming congregations, because by becoming such, the congregations necessarily put themselves outside the core tradition.) Thus we can see there's a difference between religion and spirituality.

Religion is about church; that is, it is about an institution and a set of beliefs that the institution teaches to explain and justify itself. Religion is only indirectly about good behavior and the mystical experience of God. It is more about cultural tradition, taboo, and common opinion.

What we recognize these days as spirituality is about understanding the meaning of life, living in ways consistent with enlightened vision, finding direct mystical experience of reality, resonating with the vibes, and discovering ways to serve humanity and alleviate suffering.

Scripture

The antigay interpretations of Scripture demonstrate how historical texts can be read "backward" to prove the validity of contemporary agendas. The Bible is like a Rorschach inkblot: People project into it the meaning it has for them. Much of the Bible, after all, is fairly incomprehensible. Even many of the sayings of Jesus don't make any sense. That's why preachers have to be constantly explaining how to understand the Bible.

Such preachers commonly pull quotes from Scripture out of context and combine them to make their point. Often what this produces amounts to bastardized nonsense. An example of such a line out of context is the last verse of Psalm 137: "Blessed is he who bashes the heads of your babies against a rock." How could Bible believers object to abortion when the words of the Psalmist seem to applaud infanticide? If there is truth in the Bible, it is in the overall meaning, not in the specific words. While this is obvious to anyone who knows anything about reading (even a newspaper), it seems lost on those who fetishize the Bible as totally inerrant. In context, that verse in Psalm 137 is about patriotism, not infanticide. (The babies are those of tribal enemies—so it's OK to kill them!)

The doctrine of scriptural inerrancy, which is taken to mean the Bible stories are not "myths," is actually itself a myth intended to emphasize the importance of the message. Similarly, the claim that the miraculous events described in religion *really* happened is another level of metaphor to signify the importance of the meaning of the events.

The real meaning of the idea of biblical revelation is that what's written down persists through time. (We all know this today, if for no other reason than that lawyers remind us to get everything in writing). The biblical message is that God is revealed through historical process. For the people of the era in which it was written, the Bible was the *only* book, the only thing written down; Hebrew nomads didn't carry libraries around with them. They recorded and saved the words of their collective myth because the persistence of written things over time allowed historical perspective; that is, a vantage for discovering God through time.

The myth of inerrancy is actually about writing. The myth doesn't mean the Bible is truer than other sacred texts, but rather, that everything humans learn, verify, understand, and write down is a revelation of God. The qualities of God—omniscience, immutability, omnipotence, and even beneficence—also describe the accumulation of written information. In many ways, "God" is a metaphor for science, objective fact-finding, and achieving perspective.

The nature of writing and tradition changed forever with the invention of the printing press; it's ironic that the book Gutenberg printed was the Bible, for his invention marked the end of the Bible's supremacy as the vehicle of revelation. But on a personal level, what the myth still means is that our souls "speak" to us through the events of our lives. Everything that happens to us discloses clues to who and what we really are. If we pay attention, we learn how to follow our bliss and participate in the life of God.

Many commandments in the Bible are disregarded—even by conservatives—because they are no longer applicable to modern life. The evolution of consciousness has moved on. The injunction against a man's cutting his hair (Numbers 6:5) is an obvious example: Everybody understands that was about a cultural style, not about morality. The same is true of the command against loaning money at interest (Leviticus 25:36): This ancient prohibition conflicts with our whole modern financial system, so we ignore it. Jesus unequivocally forbade divorce (Matthew 5:32), but most non-Catholic Christians disregard this commandment because it's inconsistent with today's marital lifestyles.

Modern gay-sensitive Scripture scholarship, like that in Daniel Helminiak's perennial gay best-seller, *What the Bible Really Says About Homosexuality* and John Boswell's classic *Christianity, Social Tolerance and Homosexuality,* shows the commandments against homosexual sex are also not as unequivocal as they might seem. They too reflected cultural styles, some of which are clearly outdated—like the verses that call for the stoning of homosexuals that are patently inconsistent with the spirit of religion *and* the modern concept of human rights.

Such contemporary biblical exegesis questions whether the word *homosexual* is the correct translation for ancient terms. For instance, in enumerating a list of sinners, Saint Paul used the Greek words *malakoi* and *arsenokoitai.* The first is a common adjective usually translated as *soft,* as of clothing or warm butter. The other is a street slang compound noun—found nowhere else in Scripture—which literally means "male fuckers." These are translated by such words as *homosexuals, sodomites,* or *perverts,* but is that what they meant 2,000 years ago? Translation is tricky business. What is a male fucker? Someone who fucks males? Or a male who fucks? Or something else entirely? And what's "soft" got to do with it? Maybe Saint Paul used these words to mean "lazy fuck-offs."

He might just as well have said: "Assholes aren't going to get into heaven." That wouldn't have been a denial of the Resurrection of the Body or a judgment on human anatomy. Were these slang expressions really meant as generic condemnations of homosexuals? Was Saint Paul talking about constitutionally homosexual persons? Would he have understood what that meant? Weren't the later translators just insinuating their own prejudices into texts they couldn't fully translate?

Christians ought to rejoice that modern scholarship shows that the sexist and bigoted language of the Scriptures is actually a case of mistranslation, and the early Christians weren't as unkind in their thought as we've been led to believe. Why did a religion of love and forgiveness need lists of sinners about whom to have judgmental thoughts? Jesus never gave such lists. The only people Jesus ever spoke against were the Scribes and Pharisees—the temple officials and conservative religious leaders. And why is a religion of love and forgiveness still keeping lists of sinners? (Perhaps because it's still dominated by Scribes and Pharisees!)

In any case, what difference does it make what people thought thousands of years ago? Morality has to be about how people live today, about how they can avoid causing each other pain and suffering. The Bible doesn't say anything about oil spills, air pollution, or wasting electricity. But these are moral issues today. The violation of human and civil rights is a pressing moral issue that earlier cultures wouldn't have understood. These are new ideas.

Cleanliness and Male Dominance

As gay Episcopalian priest and biblical theologian L. William Countryman shows in *Dirt, Greed & Sex: Sexual Ethics in the New Testament and Their Implications for Today,* most of the rules in the Bible govern cleanliness and ownership of property; they're not about spiritual growth or universal vision. These were partly intended to address issues of hygiene and public order for the sake of the common welfare. But they were also tools of male dominance and social control through taboo.

Taboos—belief systems—are powerful. An example of the power of taboo is the inability of most of us to eat cat food. We just can't do it, even though the cat food may have come out of the same kind of machine that in another factory is used to manufacture snacks we happily gobble up. Merely labeling the can as animal food makes it unclean and taboo. In a utopian world that truly understood the messages of Jesus, Buddha, and other spiritual leaders, compassion would be as strong a motivation as taboo. People would be as unable to hurt each other physically or emotionally as they are to eat cat food!

Modern science helps us understand the importance of hygiene. But what makes something "dirty" is its potential to expose us to harmful microorganisms, not the pleasure we derive from it. In the past, before the existence of the microscopic world was recognized, taboos and superstitions developed out of a misperception of the causes of disease.

Proponents of biblical literalism argue that the elaborate kosher laws demonstrate that God revealed good sanitary practices. Since pork can be infected with trichinosis, they say, God forbade his people to eat pork. But chicken can be infected with salmonella and beef with E. coli. Why are they kosher? If God were revealing food hygiene, he should have told his people how to identify contaminated meat or how to cure it properly. The kind of feet and number of stomachs an animal has (critical issues in the laws of kosher) have little to do with its proneness to contamination.

The objection to pork in the Bible was more likely ritualistic rather than hygienic or moral. The non-Jewish tribes the nomadic Jews sojourned among revered pork as sacred to the Goddess and consumed it ritually in her honor. It was unclean to the Jews because it was distinctively non-Jewish. Jewish law was always concerned with maintaining cultural purity and tribal identity while living among other ethnic groups.

A major objection to homosexuality was that those same Goddess-worshiping peoples practiced forms of ritual sexuality and homosexuality. These practices are referred to in the Bible as "temple prostitution." What the devotees of the Goddess experienced as sacred intercourse with the beneficent source of all life and fertility, ritually manifest in the body of a priest or priestess, the Jews derided as whoring after false idols.

Certainly the biblical distaste for homosexuality includes hygienic qualms about anal intercourse. As we noted earlier, the ancients, especially desert nomads, had no way to get anything truly clean. Body fluids were a major issue. Hence the biblical concern with menstrual blood as well.

Of course, the main objection to homosexual behavior was that a man was willingly assuming the role of a woman. That, after all, is the specific language of the command: You shall not have sex with a man as you would with a woman. That was a violation of sexual role identity and the masculine power structure.

The commandment against homosexual intercourse may have derived from a perfectly humane rule that prisoners of war not be homosexually raped. There's a long tradition of victors in battle celebrating their male prowess by fucking vanquished soldiers to disgrace and demoralize them. The behavior continues to this very day. Of course, this is not gay sexuality; this is male-dominance behavior, and it ought to be forbidden. The fact that it isn't specifically condemned elsewhere in the Bible suggests that's the meaning of the one apparently explicit prohibition against anal fucking.

Such male dominance behavior is also what the story of Sodom and Gomorrah was about. If there were actually a sex act involved at all, it would have been forcible rape and humiliation of the angelic visitors by the otherwise "straight" men of Sodom. The story of Sodom and Gomorrah is not about consensual homosexual lovemaking or even recreational sex play, but that's how the story gets interpreted out of context.

Male-dominated moral teaching is rife with homophobia. A basic purpose is to prevent men from behaving like women. The male virtues are bravado, courage, belligerence, righteousness, stoicism, unwavering conviction, and paternalistic responsibility. In practice, these mean suppressing feelings, insisting one's beliefs and opinions are right when faced with opposition and proving it by force or violence, and being selfish for one's own offspring. Homosexuality threatens male domination by prizing virtues that are womanly rather than manly: compassion, kindness, sensitivity, gentleness, egalitarianism, generosity, non-possessiveness, sophistication, cooperation, and sensuality.

Today, we can understand that commandment in Leviticus against sex with a man as with a woman to mean something we'd agree with: Homosexual men should not have sex with other men the way heterosexual men—at least in traditional societies like that of the biblical Hebrews—had sex with their women. Men should treat other men as equals—as subjects—and express affection with no ulterior purpose, no goal but love and pleasure. The Bible wouldn't have bothered to say it, but the same is true for women. Lesbians should treat other lesbians as subjects, not replicating what happens to women in male-dominant societies.

We gay men and lesbians should respect one another and never commit against each other the sins straight society accepts as inevitable consequences of gender-polarized human nature: battering, violence, sexually motivated murder, rape, pimping, routine meanness, scorn and derision for one's partner, and general disrespect and abuse of the opposite sex. This is one of the moral tenets of the gay liberation movement. It is a sign of the religious dimension of gay consciousness and gay community.

Chapter 6
Things Our Homosexuality Tells Us About the Church

Buddhism long ago recognized that myths are techniques for shaping consciousness, generating spiritual experience, and producing good vibes. Myths aren't true as descriptions of physical reality. Rather, what they describe—and modulate—is mental reality.

Modern brain research shows that spiritual practices—meditating, chanting, praying, and believing—produce changes in neuronal activity. For example, intense concentration on one's interior awareness prevents the neurons in the left superior parietal lobe's "orientation association area" from receiving enough sensory input to form the experience of a physically delimited body. Without data, the parietal lobe cannot find any boundary between self and world. The intensely focused meditator then perceives him- or herself as endless and intimately interwoven with everyone and everything else.

Such discoveries seem to verify in modern, scientific language the Buddha's insight that the gods are mental images and pedagogical mechanisms. The issue then isn't so much whether religious doctrines are "true" but whether they produce changes in consciousness (and in the brain) that make believers optimistic, creative, and loving. This shouldn't surprise followers of Jesus, for this is what he offered as the criterion for judging truth: "By their fruits, you will know them." This is also what William James, the early theorist of religion, proposed, using Francis of Assisi as his example. The truth of religious experience lies in the positive feelings and good works that result, not in the content of the story.

The validity of Saint Francis's spirituality is less dependent on whether he actually received the stigmata from Christ than on whether his ministry had a beneficial effect in the world. That to this day there are Franciscan friars living in simplicity and working to serve the poor is better proof of Francis's saintliness than, say, an archaeologist's finding the bandages Francis used to wrap his wounds or identifying nail punctures in his preserved wrist bones.

Challenging Religion

This thinking represents a real change in how people understand religion. It means the past is less important than the present and that the life of the founder of a religion is less important than the lives and behavior of his spiritual descendants. What matters is the fruit of the teaching. The truth of Christianity doesn't depend on whether Jesus rose from dead but on the history of the church and its influence on society.

The Crusades, the Inquisition, and the persecution of homosexuals go a long way toward invalidating the life and teachings of Jesus. If present Christians want to prove the validity of their religion, insisting on historical facts is much less convincing than demonstrating their love and kindness *now*. The hate and venom some Christian preachers spew at gay people suggest they're not speaking for a loving God. Indeed, that there is no such God.

Even if their behavior isn't total disproof of God, the way the Christian Churches treat homosexuals is certainly evidence they're out of touch with the wisdom of their founder. Jesus wouldn't have been antigay. He hung out with the common people: prostitutes and sinners (if there were homosexuals around, that's where they'd be). That's an essential part of the story of his ministry. Indeed, gay-sensitive scripture scholars believe the Roman centurion who asked for a miracle—and whom Jesus praised for his faith—clearly made his request on behalf of his younger homosexual lover (Matthew 8: 5–13 and Luke 7: 1–10).

In fact, Jesus seems even to have honored gayness, or at least to have offered it as a challenge. Answering the objection that his forbidding divorce discouraged men from marrying, he said, "Not all men can accept this statement, but only those to whom it has been given. For there are eunuchs who were born that way from their mother's womb; and there are eunuchs who were made eunuchs by men; and there are also eunuchs who made themselves eunuchs for the sake of the Kingdom of Heaven. He who can take it, let him take it." (Matthew 19: 11–12)

The church uses this odd saying as the basis for the obligation of celibacy, telling priests to disavow sex altogether—though, in apparent contradiction, Saint Paul called men who forbid marriage "deceitful spirits" with "doctrines of demons" (1 Timothy 4:1–3). But eunuchs aren't necessarily men who don't have sex; some male prostitutes where made eunuchs precisely so they could be more sexual. Eunuchs are men who cannot breed—or who are not so inclined. Even today, in some cultures *eunuch* is a catchall euphemism for gender-variant men of all sorts—from homosexuals to transsexuals (like the *hijras* of India). Jesus identified three kinds of eunuchs. Those born that way are intersexed individuals or obviously effeminate men who never seem interested in mating and breeding (that's how homosexuality would look in a culture without psychological sophistication or nomenclature). Eunuchs made by men are *castrati* who tend therefore to become effeminized. And those who make themselves eunuchs are us self-identified, idealistic, spiritually minded nonbreeders for the sake of the Kingdom.

Jesus specifically condemned calling other people mean names. If you call another person "Raca," you should be held guilty before the supreme court, and if you call him "fool," you're guilty enough to go to hell (Matthew 5:22). Maybe Jesus was just being hyperbolic to make a point, but maybe he really was offended by name-calling. *Raca* is translated as "good-for-nothing," perhaps equivalent to our epithets "asshole" or "faggot." Most mean names today have antihomosexual origins; curse words in the ancient world likely shared similar origins. It makes sense that Jesus wouldn't have liked homophobic speech. Jesus said, "Love your enemies; do good to those that hate you." We can presume he also meant, "Do good to those *you* hate."

If Christians really believe it's a misfortune to be gay, and if they want to save us out of love, then shouldn't they want to feel compassion for us in imitation of Christ and want to help us cope with our condition? Shouldn't they want us to be able to marry each other so that we can maintain satisfying long-term relationships and not fall into promiscuity or debauchery? Shouldn't they want us free of discrimination, antigay reprisals, and other forms of violence because they naturally abhor these things and because they see in the torture of Jesus the horror of religiosity and "righteous" violence? Shouldn't they want us to feel good about our lives because they'd want everybody to feel love for life? Shouldn't they trust our account of our own experience?

To extend the questioning further: Why do the right-wing Christians—the "Moral Majority"—oppose welfare payments and other forms of financial assistance to the poor? Jesus' major instruction for reaching the Kingdom was to sell all you have *and give to the poor* and then follow him. (Which probably meant following him out of the temple!)

How is it that, given the example of Jesus' passion and death, the primary rule of Christianity isn't "Thou shalt not torture another human being"? The icon of the Cross ought to remind Christians never to inflict pain—never to do to another person what was done to Jesus. But almost the reverse happened. Instead of condemning torture—especially torture imposed in the name of religious orthodoxy—the church authorities went into the business themselves. How could anyone have construed the Golden Rule to permit the Inquisition? Or the burning of witches—and homosexuals?

That the leadership of the Christian churches does not urge its followers to ask these kinds of questions is strong indictment against its claim to be guided by a loving God. Of course, there are "liberal Christians" and progressive congregations that *do* ask these questions and do see that a more radical form of Christianity is demanded by Jesus' gospel. But, apparently, for too many churches the Christian commandments have been lost in the mists of history.

Ugly Behavior

In late spring of 1998, just as hurricane season was starting in the south Atlantic, one of the high-profile TV evangelists issued a warning to residents of Florida. Complaining that Disney World in Orlando offered domestic-partnership benefits to its employees and sponsored a Gay Day at the amusement park, the evangelist reminded Floridians there was already a lineup of hurricanes moving westward toward Florida and that God's wrath might very well be delivered in those storms.

As it happened, the first hurricane moved toward Florida, then veered northward, bypassing Florida completely, and moved up the eastern seabord. It weakened to tropical storm status until it reached Virginia. There it stalled and revved up to hurricane force again directly over the city of Virginia Beach, the home and command center of that very evangelist's TV network.

According to modern, non-superstitious worldviews, storms are caused by atmospheric conditions. While they may be exacerbated by climatic changes like the greenhouse effect, they're not caused by God. God doesn't send natural disasters to punish sinners (Jesus himself affirmed this in Luke 13: 1–5). There's really no message to be found in that hurricane's behavior.

But according to the evangelist's worldview, the storm was going to be directed by God to punish sin. If we follow his reasoning, we have to conclude the punishment wasn't directed at Disney World or the citizens of Florida, but at him.

Shouldn't that one event have put an end to his antigay rhetoric? If he was going to take Scripture literally, shouldn't he have followed his Savior's admonition about not giving scandal to children, tied a millstone around his neck, and thrown himself into the sea? Perhaps, according to his way of seeing things, that might have saved the innocent citizens of Virginia Beach the devastation of the hurricane.

One can be relatively sure that had the hurricane hit Florida, the evangelist would have been quick to trumpet "I told you so." When it hit him instead, however, he took the storm as simple bad weather and perhaps an opportunity to ask for more donations. (Since he's a political "conservative," he doubtless believes the greenhouse effect had nothing to do with the severity of the storm.)

In 2001, as the world reeled from the September 11 terrorist attacks, this same evangelist and one of his equally famous compadres jumped the gun on popular opinion and declared that the attacks had happened because God had withdrawn his protection of the United States as punishment for the American Civil Liberties Union, feminism, abortion, and gay activism in modern culture.

In one respect they were right. Our modern society's acceptance of diversity and sexual liberation did help bring on the terrorist attack. The Islamic fundamentalist extremists are not so different from the Christian fundamentalists in their readiness to blame modernization for the problems of the world. All fundamentalists want to enforce the Law. They think that's what religion is about.

And of course, there's the Kansas-based minister with his campaign called "God Hates Fags." He brings his followers long distances cross-country to picket funerals of AIDS deaths as well as those of gay violence victims, like Matthew Shepard. They carry signs with words like MATT'S BURNING IN HELL. What in the teachings of Jesus could possibly motivate this kind of insensitive and ugly behavior?

Jesus' teaching—the thing that got him in trouble with the Pharisees, the fundamentalists of his day—was that the Law doesn't matter. To love one another is to fulfill the Law.

Interestingly, Jesus never violated the dietary laws himself. There is no story about Jesus' eating pork. The laws he objected to were laws about sex and marriage and laws about the Sabbath and going to temple. In the Book of the Acts of the Apostles, there's a story about how Saint Peter was shown in a dream that it would be OK for Christians to eat the foods forbidden to the Jews. The point of the dream was that the dietary laws were annulled by the commandment of love. Curiously, Christians dropped the rules of kosher, the laws Jesus continued to obey. But they clung to the rules about sex that he had preached against.

Paradigm Shift

The condemnation of gay people by religionists demonstrates the narrow-mindedness and provinciality of conventional religious metaphors and the need for a more enlightened vision of the purpose of life. The religious standard model looks to the past for truth. The idea of biblical revelation is that long ago God literally spoke to people and told them what to believe. Since it turns out "He" was wrong about so many things, we have to question the origins of these revelations.

Revelation does not correctly describe the solar system or the evolutionary progression of life on Earth. It doesn't describe germ theory or behavioral modification. None of the fundamental laws of nature—like Newton's laws of motion or the laws of thermodynamics—are in Scripture. The religions have been wrong about everything that can be empirically tested. Why would we think they'd be right about the things that can't be tested?

With psychological sophistication and modern awareness of how people really behave, it is obvious to us that homosexual activity is not just something people decide to do out of selfishness, meanness, or sheer sinfulness—the conclusions the TV preachers take from the Bible. But to see that requires a paradigm shift, a new way of looking at the world, one based on the reality of the present, not the rules and myths of ages past.

We see we're a different kind of human being, and we recognize this change in each other. We see sometimes—not always, of course—that we're as different from straight people of our sex as men are from women. But religion has consistently denied this by clinging to the fallacy that a homosexual orientation is nothing more than a wanton disregard for morality. At stake are the evolution of mythology and the adaptation of religious sensibilities to modern realities.

The Repression of Sexuality

Because we have no investment in the sexual status quo, we easily see that no matter how doggedly the theologians try to frame sexuality to fit into a natural-law scheme, the church's objections to abortion, contraception, and all things modern in the realm of sexuality are really founded on the presumption that sex is bad. It follows from this deluded belief that people who enjoy sexual pleasure are less virtuous (and less clean) and should suffer the consequences of their actions. These consequences may be unwanted children or sexually transmitted diseases. It doesn't really matter; both constitute disincentives to have sex. And that's what the religious people really seem to want to legislate.

The repression the church enjoins—no arousal, no genital touching, and no orgasm whatsoever except with a legally recognized spouse, in coitus, and open to the possibility of conception—creates enormous sexual frustration that does nobody any good. What are these rules for? As the gay experience of the Body Electric and such programs shows us, arousal can be a healing, inspiring, and profoundly mystical practice. That religionists have hidden this truth from us is sinful of them and hurtful to the human race. The denial of the sexuality of Jesus has wrought untold evil.

Why isn't Jesus portrayed as a mystical two-spirit person, a lover of both John and Mary Magdalene, who gathered friends and disciples together to teach them how to pleasure themselves and one another with a variety of masturbatory skills and techniques? Why don't we all naturally see that Jesus' stripping off his clothes, wrapping himself with a towel, and washing the feet of his apostles at the Last Supper was the first step in a sacred tantric orgy?

Perhaps, historically, this wasn't so. After all, Jesus was an uptight Jew struggling to teach but a modicum of liberation—he wasn't a tantric yogi. Perhaps he hadn't yet achieved for himself such a mystical vision of sexual consciousness.

But so much is mythologized about him anyway. In 2,000 years why haven't we created myths about his mystical sexuality? Of course, in all likelihood anyone who did this kind of mythologizing before the present day was burned at the stake. The irrational fear of homosexuality has prevented a Christian tradition of sacred sexuality from developing.

Priestly Pedophilia

The priestly pedophilia scandal that has rocked the Catholic Church and challenged the authority of the hierarchy tells us that there is something wrong in the Catholic teachings and doctrines about sex and embodiment. Priests are pedophiles not because pedophiles become priests but because priestly indoctrination warps men's judgment and their experience of embodiment. These men are victims of religion who end up acting in grossly inappropriate ways without a conscious understanding of what they're doing.

These days, with the number of men joining the clergy dramatically decreasing, the church has sought recruits among the adult population. These so-called "late vocations" may include men who are attracted to the priesthood because of the power it gives them over vulnerable children. But they're not most priests. Most priests today joined at the end of parochial school or high school when they were 13 or 17 years of age. Such earnest young men are driven by naive zeal, selfless generosity, and the tenets of Catholic doctrine to renounce the things of the flesh entirely for the sake of God's immaterial, ethereal Kingdom. These boys don't join the priesthood because they think it will be a good way to get sex. If anything, they believe they will be able to give up sex entirely.

The scandal that caused the Vatican to call the American bishops to Rome hit the news at a time when there'd just been a series of high-profile cases involving the kidnap and murder of young girls. These truly horrific, senseless, and tragic (and heterosexual) offenses outraged the public over sex crimes against children. It was in this context that priestly misconduct made headlines.

But the media-driven sensationalism—and the legal claims for huge settlements of church money—distort the reality of priestly "pedophilia." Ephebophilia—love of postpubescent teenagers—might be a more apt term for what some of the priests were doing. This particular form of love reflects the mentoring pattern that some cultures—classical Greece the usual example—institutionalized as honorable and beneficial. (Of course, even so, you have to wonder how these priests could have been so ignorant of the laws governing the age of consent and the rules of professional ethics.) In the media *and in court,* the sexual gestures of the accused priest are characterized as ravishment and child-rape to evoke images of forceful penetration—what frustrated, angry adult males do to females. Heterosexual dynamics get projected onto the situation, because the media, the courts, and the public don't understand homosexual sexual dynamics.

With our understanding, we may see that while some of these acts truly are crimes of rape and molestation, often they are far more innocent, well-intentioned, if terribly misguided, gestures of affection. More likely, we can imagine that these adult priests, obsessed with religious imagery and driven by it to suppress sexual feelings, had come to revere the innocence of the young boys in their care. They see in those boys their own lost boyish innocence. They covet that innocence. And they desire the boy who incarnates it. They likely experience their desire as something totally different from sex, perhaps even as something holy. It certainly isn't the heterosexuality they vowed to abjure. They may project onto a boy serving at their altar that this innocent youth too has a religious vocation, and may think their affection a sign of God's electing the boy to the next generation of priesthood. Drawn by the vision of Christ in the boy, they reach out to touch that vision and find themselves totally unprepared for the sexual emotions and compulsions that follow.

Media attention has made it appear that those coming forward to report that years ago they were traumatized by the homosexual advances of priests and to sue the church for damages are now heterosexual adult men. In fact, about half of the victims who've organized to challenge the church are women. And of course, some of the victims are gay, but they're far from center stage. Were all gay adults similarly traumatized? Or were they instead liberated? There would be little media interest in reporting the story of a man who had been the object of an advance by a creepy priest but who also admitted he had a good attitude about his sexuality, bore no ill will toward the priest, and had no desire to claim money from the priest's diocese.

A question that remains unanswered—and maybe unanswerable—is whether priests and other religious have always been pedophiles. Catholic seminarians privately joke about the so-called *jus primae noctis* ("right of the first night"), according to which, supposedly, in ancient times the feudal lord or *the presiding priest* had the prerogative to sexually initiate a virgin bride on the first night of her marriage. Perhaps one of the traditional functions of the priesthood was to initiate young people into sexuality. That's not to defend it, just to question what's actually been going on.

It's a joke in modern American society that parents can't bring themselves even to have the "birds-and-the-bees talk." They become tongue-tied by their reluctance to see their beloved babies grow up to sexual adulthood and by their own sexual awareness of their children. Parents are confronted with feelings that cannot be allowed into consciousness. Fathers can't initiate their sons into masturbation. Mothers can't show their daughters how to feel the pleasure their bodies are capable of experiencing.

Sexual maturity ends the innocence of childhood; sexual, emotional, and relational issues displace the simple concerns of the playroom. Delaying that is probably a boon to the children and an aid to their maturation. But they *are* going to become aware of their physical urges. Their genital organs *are* going to mature. That's inevitable. So who should teach sons and daughters how to touch themselves and to celebrate human incarnation in feeling flesh? Shouldn't it be the priests? Who better understands how to place all these feelings in the context of ego-transcending love? Who better to tell boys how to bring themselves to orgasm without snickering and embarrassment? Who better to teach them—at the proper age, of course—the Body Electric techniques for finding ecstasy in sexual arousal?

Obviously it isn't going to be the Catholic priests of today's Catholic Church, with its antisexual, homophobia-justifying agenda. To find such priest-initiators we have to recall those hunter-gatherer days when the religions worshiped the Great Mother and celebrated her mysteries with reverent orgies and transcendence-inducing orgasms. To find such priests, perhaps we have to create a metaphorical history of such a matriarchal time. Perhaps we need a radically new religion.

Considering the trauma, belligerence, and violence that our current antisexual, patriarchal religions have produced, perhaps it's not just the altar boys who've been abused by the priests. All of us have had the wool pulled over our eyes.

Gay Priests

The ecclesiastical solution to the scandal has been to blame homosexuals in the priesthood and to act surprised that there are such men in their midst. Of course there are homosexuals in the priesthood. Priests are likely to be gay. They are supposed to exemplify self-sacrifice, generosity, sensitivity, kindness, and noncompetitiveness—all the traits of gay men.

Celibacy is said to keep homosexuals out of the church,

but celibacy is actually not the renunciation of sex but of marriage and child rearing. Sex is only indirectly forbidden because, according to Catholic doctrine, sex is only lawful in the state of marriage. Celibacy originated in the need to avoid widows and children becoming the responsibility of the institution. Church property couldn't be allowed to pass through inheritance outside the church. Priests can't have heirs.

Homosexuals enter the priesthood because they aren't motivated to pursue sex with women, marriage, or parenthood. They're just the kind of men the church needs. They're drawn to the religious life because homosexuals are basically sensitive and kind and because the church provides the doctrinal explanation for their disinclination toward heterosexual sex. The Catholic Church helpfully declares that sex is the greatest temptation and boys shouldn't even look at girls for fear of arousing sinful passions. Is it any wonder young, unaware homosexuals seek refuge in the church?

To solve the pedophilia problem, the church needs to offer a sex-positive vision, a doctrine of sexual pleasure that allows priests to form sexual bonds with women, perhaps women priests—or with other conscious gay adult men—and that utilizes modern technologies to prevent conception. The church needs to embrace masturbation (perhaps as meditative, spiritual practice—the way some modern gay men are doing), contraception, even abortion in the service of body-positive, celibate (i.e., childless) sex lives *for* priests.

Instead, church authorities address the scandal by driving out the openly gay, sexually aware priests. They say they're getting rid of the bad apples, leaving only properly repressed heterosexuals in the ranks. This leaves the church with the even more confused, conflicted, repressed men in various stages of nailing shut their closet doors. Proclamations of the evil and inherent disorderedness of conscious gay people ring with hypocrisy.

Everybody sees that the real "crime" is the hierarchical cover-up. The bishops lied and shielded the child abusers to protect their own public image and fund-raising abilities. Of course, in part, this is a result of the same kind of loyalty that causes police officers to protect other police officers accused of wrongdoing. But perhaps it's also a result of the bishops' innate understanding that the sins of the priests often weren't as heinous as the scandal-mongering media have led the public to believe.

But the bishops are in great part responsible for the public's hysteria, and the hysteria indeed makes the priests' behavior heinous and its consequences traumatizing. (Secrecy and cover-up always make sexual abuse far more emotionally damaging than the actual act of sex itself.) Our awareness of the secret homosexual slant to things, and our own understanding of the innocence of homosexual affections, allow us to see that the bishops demonstrate understanding and sympathy for the pedophile priests. Perhaps the bishops see this is not something new and that the pedophile priests' behavior, though not acceptable, is at least "understandable."

But then instead of finding somebody to blame, why don't the bishops defuse the hysteria by telling the truth about homosexuality? As church historian Mark Jordan describes in *The Silence of Sodom,* the real crime is that the church knows it's a gay institution and understands the homosexual peccadillos of its priests while fiercely denying the truth and ratcheting up its rhetoric against homosexuality to bolster the denials. The church's sin is being soft on conflicted, closeted homosexuals in its midst while being hard on open, self-affirming gay people in modern, secular society. The church opposes gay rights, fights gay marriage, objects to safe-sex education, and condemns homosexuality as unnatural and disordered—all to protect its own secret.

Priests serving in the church, and especially idealistic young seminarians, identify themselves as gay not in rebellion to church authority but out of personal integrity. They're not necessarily violating their vows: One can be openly gay and proud *and* be sexually continent. For men (and women) in the church, it's an act of courage, psychological health, and honesty to tell the truth—to themselves, to their brothers or sisters in religious community, and to God. Openly gay priests and seminarians aren't disobedient; they're heroic. They're telling that truth about the emperor's new clothes. They are not the ones who need to be disciplined.

But maybe gay priests *should* leave the church—for their own sake. Conventional religion—with its antiquated understanding of human psychology, rigid rules of social behavior, and neurosis-inducing attitudes toward embodiment—is not the place for gay men. Gay men are spiritual, and spiritual men are usually gay. These men deserve a religion that enables them to flourish as the saints they are, not one that cripples their sexuality and shapes them into predators of little boys. What a terrible waste of good gay lives!

Talent for Religion

There are certain talents that seem to come with being gay: the ability to decorate a room or to assemble an outfit, for example. These talents come from what we earlier called gay intuition. Also among these gay talents are mythopoesis, religion, and the creation of liturgy and ritual.

Throughout recorded history, gay men have organized rituals and choreographed events. Gay men have been the

shamans who organized tribal dances and the trouba-
dours—the Mattachines—who went from town to town
putting on performances and sharing news and gossip.
We've been the playwrights, poets, magicians, dancers, and
priests. Our modern gay culture still creates rituals: deeply
moving AIDS memorials, innovative Q-spirit "techno-masses,"
psychotherapeutic Gay Spirit Visions and Billy Club "heart
circles," whimsical Radical Faerie extravaganzas and sol-
stice/equinox celebrations, and spectacular disco rites to
mark the migration of the Manhattan club scene to Fire
Island for the summer season.

Rituals are good for people—they create social interaction. They bring people together around shared hopes and
intentions. In the modern world, religious rituals are often
the only opportunity most people have to sing with others.
Rituals have the power to stir deep emotions and to inspire;
singing can alter consciousness. But they need to be understood for what they are, not for what they pretend to be.
The pretending is part of the ritual; it activates their power.
But its power is in the mind. The power of a ritual comes
from within the ritual, not from whether an observer-god is
pleased—or displeased—with the details of its performance
or whether some sort of invisible grace or merit is conveyed.
For example: The purpose of a rain dance was to bring the
members of the tribe together to voice their common concern about the scarcity of food and water. They would revel
in the good feelings that came from dancing together and
share scarce supplies with the people in the greatest need.
The value of the dance didn't necessarily hinge on whether
it rained the next day.

Similarly, church has a positive social role. For many people
its main function is as much social as spiritual: It's a way to meet
people, to share experiences and concerns with friends and

neighbors. In the gay world, the Metropolitan Community Church (and local variations and spin-offs) provides an occasion for spiritually inclined folks to meet and form friendships with kindred souls outside the sex-charged context of gay commercial milieus. Part of the beauty of MCC is its freedom from orthodoxy. MCCers do not find themselves at odds with one another or with other religions (except regarding homosexuality, of course). There's no reason for MCC to divide into sects—like mainstream Christianity, which *does* teach orthodoxy. MCCers don't split off because one group believes in transubstantiation, another in consubstantiation, and another that the Eucharist is allegorical. It doesn't matter. What holds the MCC together is gay identity, not doctrinal agreement.

Religion is wonderful. It can bring people joy. But religion is for people, not God.

Two-Spirits and Saints

The presence of gay people in religion is not a surprise. As research like that of gay anthropologists Walter L. Williams and Will Roscoe shows, Native American cultures revered people with anomalous sexuality. These people were called by various names by different tribes. By white men they were called *berdache*—a derogatory term meaning "bottom" in homosexual sex. Contemporary gay Native Americans have coined the more respectful term "two-spirits" to highlight a notion common to most tribes—that these people are blessed with both a female spirit and a male spirit, hence their blurring of sex roles.

Two-spirits were sometimes identified in a ceremony called the Bow or the Basket. Children who showed signs of being two-spirited had to choose between manly things and womanly things; sometimes they had to dash into a burning tepee or hut to save what was most important. The tribe recognized them as two-spirits if they chose objects associated with the opposite sex: boys who chose basket-weaving materials or girls who chose weapons.

Their sexual anomaly represented spiritual election. Some two-spirit people grew up to become healers, medicine people, visionaries, and tribal leaders. They also often served as ambassadors to other tribes because they were good at tact and protocol.

That most gay people live good, socially enriching lives—some of us are truly modern-day saints—demonstrates that ethical living does not require church membership, belief in a god (Judeo-Christian or otherwise), or fear of hell. Love and empathy motivate people to do good. People who feel other people's pain don't cause pain. Compassion, not fear of punishment or concern for taboo violation, should guide morality.

Don't you want everybody to be safe and happy? Isn't that what your gayness urges—happiness, satisfaction, sexual pleasure, and beauty for you and for everybody else? When everybody else's pleasure is your pleasure, there is no competition. No one is excluded. Your desire not to be excluded includes everybody else. Isn't this what religion should be teaching everyone to feel?

Desensitizing the World

An enormous amount of hidden homosexual activity goes on in society—in the priesthood, the army, the Boy Scouts, Masonic lodges, and in the steam rooms of the nation's gyms and YMCAs. And straight men account for an awful lot of this hidden sex. The shame they feel produces many of the problems the world suffers.

Straight men—and closeted homosexuals—protect their

secret (especially from themselves) by being antigay. This is most obvious in the church. All the bishops and ministers who preach against gay rights *look* gay; they smirk, smile, prance, and purse their lips in ways that mimic stereotypical homosexual mannerisms. Their repressed homosexuality pushes its way to the surface to belie the rhetoric.

If they were a little less homophobic and ashamed of their sexuality—and their homosexuality—this would be a calmer, more peaceful world. The most important function of gay liberation may be to help the mainstream population feel more comfortable and less intimidated by the idea of homosexuality. You can see this is happening. The appearance of gay themes in TV and the arts as well as the widespread fascination with drag and other gender-role violations indicate that straight people are becoming more enlightened. It's also a sign that gay people are increasingly accepted as part of the complex human world and loved as friends, relatives, and neighbors.

As straight people get used to hearing about gay people's issues, their own tight, repressive mechanisms relax. And everybody gets to have a better time. That's a way of transforming the world.

Spirituality: A Higher Order of Consciousness

To understand things, we think of them in terms of other things; we create associations and metaphors. The essence of metaphor is simile: This is like that. A car that uses excessive gasoline is a gas guzzler. It doesn't do this literally but figuratively—metaphorically. It's *like* the car drank the gas thirstily. The myth that there is a God watching us, urging us to be obedient, and answering requests—like a human father—doesn't mean there really *is* such a paternal character in heaven somewhere. Rather, it means life should be lived *like* there were such a father: that is, with confidence, hope, and good expectations. Our prayers may be answered, but not because

God has decided to help, but because intentions and expectations have power to fulfill themselves. The myth is really about the power of intention.

Being conscious *is* thinking metaphorically. This is how we learn new things and expand our awareness. We associate new things with previous things: We compare and contrast, and we explain things to ourselves in terms of things we already know. In the physical matter of the brain, dendrites grow and form connections with other nerve cells, developing neural pathways from one thought to another. The self-awareness of this process is what we call consciousness.

Spirituality is a higher order of consciousness than religion, though spirituality can include religion. Indeed, spiritual practice is the real basis of religion. Religion is one of the clues to the nature of consciousness. Spiritual maturation calls for rising above religion, seeing the metaphors, understanding their meaning, and not just taking them at face value. This is not necessarily rejecting religion. In fact, it means to comprehend it even more fully. The proper progression of the spiritual life leads one *beyond* religion. That may or may not entail leaving religion behind. One can remain within the liturgical congregation of the church. But spiritual maturation necessarily raises one above literal belief.

In the meaning of the famous Zen aphorism, "The finger pointing at the moon is not the moon," so religion is not spirituality. We might say spirituality is consciousness giving clues to itself about what it really is.

The insight of spirituality is that truth is multiple and transcends the distinctions created by human culture, history, and geography. To understand this requires rising above the quicksand of tradition in order to understand what the myth of God is really about and to imagine God for today's world.

Chapter 7
Things Our Homosexuality Tells Us About God

One of the first things our experience as homosexuals tells us is that if God is loving, he wouldn't have made us gay, given us such magnificent sexual urges, and then commanded us not to follow them. That just doesn't make sense. Our sexual frustration would not make God happy. It wouldn't make the world better. Why would anybody want to love a God who'd do something like that? That God couldn't exist.

But there is no doubt God exists. *God* is a word likely to appear in almost every book in the library; almost everybody uses it at least once a day. So that's to say there is no doubt God exists as a human idea. Carl Jung, the psychoanalyst most interested in understanding religion and the spiritual component of the human psyche, called this the *imago Dei,* the image of God. This clearly exists, influences people's behavior, and shapes history.

The popular religions of the West—Judaism, Islam, and Christianity—propose the metaphor of an omniscient, personal God to explain human life and to enforce a set of behavioral standards. Seen from a perspective over and above the metaphor of religion, this proposition looks primitive and anthropomorphic—male dominance writ large across the universe. The traditional idea of the personal God is too megalomaniacal, too egotistical, and too mythological—too anthropomorphic—to make much sense to the modern mind.

Anthropomorphism is a ubiquitous human trait: We

name our animals. Some of us even name our cars and refer to them as though they were personal beings. We all enjoy the joke. We call inanimate objects by personal pronouns and assign gender, even though there is nothing sexual about them (ships, for instance, are referred to with feminine pronouns). We even assign human names to hurricanes.

It's fun to imagine human traits in nature, to project personality into natural processes. We might anthropomorphize a tree by imagining a kind of awareness within the tree that allows it to make decisions the way a human being does. We might even think about how water freezes or how a machine works by imagining that it responds to its environment the way a human would: We say "Water wants to freeze when it gets this cold" or "The car is asking for an oil change." But because we're able to understand this psychological process, we don't *literally* believe it. Instead, we *figuratively* believe it. This is how God is personal.

Understanding that God is figuratively, but not literally, a personal being is not being antireligious. It is a more inclusive realization, from a higher perspective, and more enlightened. God need not be personal to be a source of meaning for human beings, a reason for living, or an ethical motivation. God as a universal process of which we are all a part might, in fact, be a better motivator and better inspiration.

Unfortunately, too often popular religion keeps its adherents naive. In fact, the very basis of most American Protestant spiritualities is the cultivation of "a personal relationship with Jesus." You're supposed to conceive of and relate to God as a person who lived in history and conquered death so he could remain a person with whom you could have a personal relationship. No matter how you understand it, though, that personal Jesus is in your mind. It's what you imagine the historical character—whom you have never actually met— would be like if you could meet him. The preachers who have a church to operate are more than happy to tell you what he'd be like, of course.

God Is in the Mind

The purpose of religion is not to appease or pleasure a personal God but to change human experience and to expand *our* perceptions of what life is about. God is a metaphor for greater being and further evolution of consciousness. In fact, God is the mind. This is not really a derogation of God. Indeed, in a way, it's a proof of God. But it does move God out of the heavenly throne room and into psychological and cerebral space.

God is an artifact of the brain structures and neuronal activity of the human mind because the brain is the physical manifestation of consciousness and is "programmed" with clues to what consciousness really is. God is a clue the brain gives itself to its own future. As Arthur C. Clarke proposed, the idea of God predicts—and enables—the evolution of greater consciousness and reveals our roles as conscious beings in the universe.

The image of God you hold in mind and believe affects how you live and how you feel about life. Indeed, the point of believing in God is to shape how you live and to make your experience of life meaningful and joyful. Some images and metaphors are more effective at conveying this than others.

Metaphors for God

It makes sense to say God is like America. We Americans are part of America. We can truly say we love being Americans and we love America. But America is not a personal being. The personality we might imagine in thinking about "the national character," symbolized by the figure of Uncle Sam and historically associated with George

Washington, is really in us, not *out there*. We don't pray to America or expect America to work miracles on our behalf out of personal concern for us as individuals, but we do understand that the American experiment in democracy has granted us virtually miraculous boons. We might give our allegiance to America, devote our labor to making America successful, and even die to defend her (note the personal pronoun).

To extend the analogy: Just as we see that our government isn't America, so we see that religion and the church aren't God. Opposing the government by mobilizing to protest governmental error and abuse can be a way to show patriotism and to force government to adapt and address real problems. We're better Americans because we want change. In the same way, we're better lovers of God because we mobilize to protest the churches and seek to force religion to adapt and re-create itself—and its image of God—for the modern world.

God Is Love

Saint John the Evangelist, who called himself Jesus' beloved, said: "God is Love." Perhaps he had experienced an intense realization of the *imago Dei* through his relationship with Jesus.

Love is an abstraction, an idea about an experience, and an interpretation of deep human feelings and psychological bonds. Love is not a personal being. The notion that our emotional attraction to other people is caused by arrows shot by Cupid is clearly a metaphor. There is no personal Cupid. Love is recognizing a common identity with another person and therefore wanting the person to be part of your life. You feel a connection. You care. It is recognition in the other of common identity in the greater Self—which is metaphorized as God.

The desire to be one with God is the desire to be loved, an actual physical necessity for conscious beings, just like the necessity of food or air. That's why God is metaphorized so commonly as both food and breath. God *is* love. That doesn't mean God is a personal being who experiences emotional attractions and feels affection and desire. Rather, it means the feelings that we have as human beings when we care about other people are participation in the universe's longing for harmony and abundant life. For love is the desire for harmony, for the smooth unfolding of change (i.e., the expansion of space-time). Love is the intention that there be no suffering and the motivation, out of compassion and enlightened self-interest, to help others who are suffering.

The need to be loved—to be touched—is part of the process by which the nervous system grows in the matrix of energy fields generated by other beings. Without touch, human children wither and die just as if they had been deprived of sustenance. The desire to touch and to be touched is not an urge born of selfishness and ungodly lust; rather, it is the longing of life to live and be healthy—and to participate in the generation of energy fields. The satisfaction of the desire to be touched and loved *is* God.

Love can be sparked by a variety of factors: common interests, mutual devotion to a cause, friendship, or kinship. Of course, in modern American culture, love usually refers specifically to sexual attraction and to familial bonds.

The metaphor *God is love* means that the universe intends for life to succeed and for human beings to flourish. We can *see* that "God is love": Everywhere life blossoms. The Earth is verdant and fertile. With each breath every creature on the planet sings out the song of joy at being alive. Surely, life intends to thrive and be happy—it is the expression of the cosmic expansion of matter and consciousness. Indeed, *God is love* is a metaphor for the expanding cosmos. You might say the Big Bang was God's paroxysm of passion for existence.

Therefore, to love all humankind means to find common identity with all other inhabitants of planet Earth. *God is love* enjoins us to find God in that space in human consciousness where goodwill naturally arises. It is the space beyond right and wrong, just and unjust, deserving and undeserving— beyond judging. It's willing happiness and good fortune for all beings, just because all beings are interconnected in such a way as to form the Self of the universe.

God as Music

You might also say God is like a symphony orchestra, a lovely and evocative metaphor. An orchestra or a chorale is made up of many individuals. Each person plays his instrument or modulates her voice according to individual style. When everyone performs together, another kind of being is created: the music. The music isn't personal, but it has a life of its own. Members of the orchestra or the chorale respond to cues from one another and from the conductor. Orchestras and chorales usually follow printed and rehearsed music, but imagine a jam session in which each musician expresses his or her feelings and musical perceptions while listening to and responding to the expressions of all the others. Imagine the orchestra swelling to grand expressions of joy and delight or sinking to deep, resonant, soft tones of melancholy and nostalgia. The music begins to move of itself. The collective activity of the orchestra or the chorus of voices communicates at a higher level than the individuals. It isn't personal, but it conveys deeply personal sensibilities. It inspires and motivates the musicians and their audience. It calls individuals together to synchronize and to become something beyond themselves, something multidimensional at the level of mind and spirit. In playing their music, the individuals transcend themselves and enter the music, just as praying souls aspire to enter communion with God.

Our lives are the music of Planet Earth. God is the voice

with which we all sing. No wonder singing is one of the most common—and beloved—forms of worship!

If God is like a symphony orchestra in a grand improvisational jam session, then the great mythological and cultural traditions are like the recurrent themes, leitmotifs, and familiar melodies by which the orchestra gives itself cues and clues to where the music's going.

God as Mystery

Yet another metaphor for God is mystery: the question that cannot be answered. For the ancients, one of the primary functions of religion was to provide answers to such questions. They didn't understand how much of anything worked, so there were many questions without answers. God was generally the answer.

Today, science answers those questions: the origin of the universe, the workings of the body, the experience of mind. Yet there are still things inexplicable. There are what can be called "fringe phenomena": alien abduction, UFOs, apparitions of the Blessed Virgin Mary, sightings of Bigfoot, miraculous healings, crop circles, telepathy, clairvoyance, out-of-body experience, bizarre coincidences, and also just the routine synchronicities, mystical raptures, and miracles of everyday life. These point to a complexity of the universe—and consciousness—far beyond that of the common paradigm.

Most people in modern America live in a pretty ordinary world. Things fit their conception of reality. But scattered among them are people having totally different experiences of the world. Scattered among them, there are people who are nightly being visited by aliens or by angels or soul-traveling out of body to other realms. To most people gay life seems just as bizarre and outré as alien visitors and the like. We are a fringe phenomenon.

Our experience on the fringe of society shows us that just

as to explain sexuality fully you also have to explain homosexuality, so to explain the nature of reality fully you have to be able to explain the various fringe phenomena that don't fit the ordinary model. You have to expand your paradigm. These phenomena demonstrate that different people live in different universes, that things are stranger than they seem.

People who've experienced fringe phenomena find these events just as compelling and life-changing as we find our homosexuality. Many marginalized people, like many of us, develop tunnel vision because of the compelling nature of their fringe experiences. Instead of discerning the connections among all of them, most become fixated on their own experience. Because we are a fringe phenomenon in human society—ignored, dismissed, or dissed by most people—we can understand how important fringe phenomena can be as pointers toward the nature of consciousness and God. We need to see these phenomena are all of a piece: They are all clues, all metaphors for consciousness. They work together to reveal consciousness to itself as something marvelous, creative, and transcendent.

These phenomena show us how the consciousness in each of us creates his or her own world. We should be interested in these phenomena because they also help us to create new myth. In fact, they are a major component of modern-day myths. In popular films and novels, fictional stories of supernatural and paranormal happenings both entertain and convey important messages.

Fringe phenomena are in some ways the most important events in the world. They reveal that there's more to life than meets the eye. They reveal the multidimensionality of the universe. They reveal that the common paradigm has to be forced open to include a bigger vision of reality.

Less attached to the way things are, gay people can more readily adopt a radically new paradigm. Gayness stimulates us to be more expansive and inclusive thinkers.

God as Space

Perhaps the best metaphor for God is space. The universe that astronomy has discovered in the last 50 years—especially since the launching of the Hubble telescope—is aweinspiring beyond any hoary description of God and the Heavenly Hosts. We now understand that space extends out billions of light-years and that it's almost completely empty. The advances in quantum physics that have accompanied recent astronomical discoveries reveal that within the matter scattered through cosmic space, there is also incredible emptiness. That very emptiness is like God, for that empty space is the field of infinite possibility. Matter, energy, and space-time itself bubble up from the quantum foam. Through vast distances of empty potentiality, matter comes into existence and over measureless stretches of time becomes conscious, self-aware. We ourselves are woven out of the fabric of space.

And this is a wonder we can *see*. We can look out at the universe—even with the naked eye—and feel the profundity. Especially at sunrise and sunset, we can observe how the massive spheres of Earth, Sun, and Moon move in ponderous cadence. We feel the immensity of it all. We look on the face of this God and naturally rejoice to be alive.

Within the incredible vastness and infinite smallness that human consciousness has discovered, the best and clearest image of God is the Sun. The Sun is God; everyone can see that. From our star pours forth all the energy that has created life on Earth. From the Sun—without any preferences, opinions, or judgments—comes our life, our food and drink, and the natural world around us. The Sun imparts everything—even the molecules and atoms that compose our physical bodies.

The Sun is the perfect symbol of love. It has no personal stake in the matter. It just keeps shining.

God as Nonpersonal

The way you know God is by your experience of the world. If God is love, then the way you experience God in your life is as the love in your life. God loves you through the people who love you, wrap their arms around you, and show you affection. All the affection you get in this life comes from God—that's what God is. God manifests to you as the human beings in your life. God makes love to you as your lover making love to you.

Your lover—a longtime committed partner or the pretty man who has just introduced himself to you—is God appearing in your life. Rather than taking us away from matters spiritual, our sexuality dramatizes our place in spiritual reality, fills us with affirmation, allays our fears, emboldens us to live our lives as fully as we can, and frees us from life-restricting guilt. Almost automatically, we want others to desire us, to want to take us in their arms, hold us, and cherish our bodies. We want that experience for others as well—then we love as God loves: willing happiness and harmony for everybody. This God isn't personal but manifests as personal in every person you meet.

Problems arise from the image of God as a personal, patriarchal entity who cares whether he's loved and worshiped, who expects supplication, and who makes arbitrary interventions in people's lives. That kind of personal God generates neurosis. Life becomes an effort to persuade this elusive, non-forthcoming deity to demonstrate his love by answering prayers. As Sigmund Freud observed, the personal God is a projection of an individual's parents, with all the confusion and ambivalence that arise within a family. The personal God loves *and* hates. He can—and apparently does—answer prayers arbitrarily and send punishment randomly. He behaves like a terrorist, scaring people into submission.

There is a warlike quality in both Judeo-Christianity and

Islam—the religions of the Book and of the personal God. This is a product of the missionary teachings of the religions. "Go forth and preach to all men and convert them to my message," say both Jesus and Mohammed.

In Islam this belligerent missionary zeal is redoubled by the Muslim concern with racial/tribal identity and the belief that authority and government derive from that tribal identity. Christianity suffers less from this because it deliberately broke with tribal identity as it spread into pluralistic Europe. But it shares with Islam the belief that everybody should be converted.

The missionary zeal of Christianity and Islam comes from the patriarchal commitment to rigid notions of right and wrong. This zealousness accounts for the note of finality in both religions: Jesus is "the *only* begotten Son of God" and Mohammed is "the *Last* Prophet."

But those statements weren't really meant to discount all other possibilities for the future or to constrain God from ever revealing Himself again. They were cultural hyperboles intended to honor Jesus and Mohammed—statements about the faith of the original followers of these prophets. The missionary zeal obscures this context and gives the words a meaning inconsistent with the spiritual experience the founders were talking about. It made it into something personal, not mystical.

Buddhism is a missionary religion, but it has no personal God. Its mission comes not from its believing it's right but from its compassion for suffering. Buddhism does not have a belligerent side.

The idea of a nonpersonal God strikes many religious people as antireligious or atheistic. In reality, such a nonpersonal God is the object of religious belief for most people on Earth. In the great religions of the East, God and the gods are generally not personal; rather, they are elements of nature and forces within human personality. Buddhism specifically denies the existence of personal gods and for this reason is called "nontheist."

Buddhist teaching is not that there are no higher levels of consciousness or no other sorts of beings in the universe, but that these beings have no significance for the human quest for fulfillment and enlightenment. The gods have nothing to do with us or our effort to live right lives. More importantly, the personalities people imagine in the gods are projections of their own personalities. That's the key Buddhist insight: Gods as personalities exist in the human mind. There is much more in the universe than just human consciousness, but whatever we think about it, we're always still inside our own heads.

However, the nonpersonal God isn't entirely in the mind. It exists as the laws and dynamics of the universe. God is analogous to the laws of mathematics: $2 + 2 = 4$; $C = 2\pi r$. These are exact relations. They are absolute and immutable truths. These and other mathematical relations determine the shape of the universe. Out of them creation emerged. But there's nothing personal about them. Even the personal God envisioned by Judeo-Christianity is subject to them; with all Yahweh's omnipotence, even He cannot draw a circle with a circumference unequal to $2\pi r$. (Note the Bible's mathematical "error" in 2 Chronicles 4:2.)

One of the traditional Christian proofs for the existence of God is the order in the universe. It's not all chaos. The polemicists argue that this demonstrates the existence of a conscious Entity who planned everything and keeps it all in good working order. In fact, the order in the universe is a product of the laws of mathematics. No conscious Entity could have come up with a different set of mathematical laws. Perhaps God could have created the Earth with a different average climate or a different number of moons in the sky. But He couldn't have created different mathematical relations or changed the laws of physics that follow from them.

Anthropomorphizing the laws of math and physics gives

rise to the personal God. As previously observed, human beings have a penchant for anthropomorphization. We like imagining and projecting personality into the world around us. The problem with anthropomorphization is that it suggests that the personality traits of unreliability, finickiness, changeableness, and arbitrariness—the marks of human neuroses—exist outside.

You don't pray to mathematics to make your income tax calculations come out correctly. Engineers don't perform rituals in honor of mathematics to assure that the bridges they build won't collapse. God is love, but you don't pray to Love to solve a problem in your relationship with your lover. As Buddha would say, you're on your own. *You* have to solve the problem. *You* have to get the tax calculations correct. The engineer in charge of the bridge has to make sure his engineering is right. These outcomes have nothing to do with how ardently you plead to a personal being.

Personal Relationship With a Nonpersonal God

Though God is beyond personality, we can still have a personal relationship with God. With our talent for "double vision," we can understand there is no conflict between believing God is personal and understanding God is nonpersonal. The question then is not "Do you believe in God?" but "How would you like to imagine God?" We can imagine God as personal. We can talk to God in our minds. In essence, we can talk to life. Such prayer is a way to clarify our hopes and intentions and to understand what our lives mean.

We find God—life—replying to us in the events of our lives, especially in unexpected, surprising, and synchronistic, coincidental events, especially in those moments that cause us to experience wonder and to be glad to be alive. Experiences of love and sex are important among these. Our lives speak to us through those to whom we are attracted, who cause us to feel the pang of beauty. It is, after all, from among these people that a true love might appear to change our destiny by blending his or her life with ours. Our prayers are answered as our lives. Our effort to relate to God is our way of understanding what our lives are telling us.

There are two ways we relate to God: God within us and ourselves within God. God is within us in the sense that God is a figure in personal psychology (which is shaped by our experience of our parents). We pray to God within our minds. We carry on internal dialogues. The internal image we anthropomorphize is in us.

We are within God in the sense that God is a metaphor for the universal or planetary process, the "greater consciousness" that comprises all the individual consciousnesses of human beings. We are organs of God. God is not self-aware in the way we are. Indeed, God's self-awareness *is* our awareness of God. Thus God within *is* God without.

If we anthropomorphize God in order to have a personal relationship, we must take responsibility for what we imagine this God desires and values. We have to be mindful that this God is a projection of our own minds. The messages that come from this God are really coming from our own deepest Self, not from some external Being. This configuration requires the ability to hold two seemingly contrary thoughts in mind at once. We are responsible for the kind of God we create. After all, how we envision God determines the universe we inhabit. How we envision God can be a self-fulfilling prophecy.

Afterlife

The various religions' visions of God and the universe are conveyed in their myths of afterlife. Afterlife mythology exemplifies a tradition's metaphysical concept of the universe: the three-layer cake model of heaven-earth-hell or the "transmigrating souls" model of reincarnation.

It's comforting to imagine that people don't really die but just depart for another kind of existence. Our experience of AIDS has given most of us a premature lesson in this. Especially when we're mourning the death of a loved one or facing a frightening medical prognosis, it helps to think death isn't an end. Belief in afterlife is considered one of the first signs that primitive human beings had begun to develop self-awareness and to create religion.

The afterlife most of us in modern America grew up believing in, however, doesn't really make much sense. It's more about the ego's fears than about the supernatural dimensions of the universe. Does it really make sense—or seem comforting—that after death each human being will continue to mull over the events of his or her 70 or 80 years of life on Earth for the duration of the cosmos? That would make a boring hell out of heaven.

The afterlife myths that most old-time religions teach just keep you stuck in ego. The promise of reward in heaven promotes the kind of fanaticism and hatred for life—and for the present—that allows suicide bombers and cultic death pacts. The part of us that doesn't want to die and doesn't want others to die is our egos, the part of us that keeps us feeling separate from the world. The part of us that transcends death is not the ego but the greater consciousness of which ego is but a passing manifestation. The part of us that transcends death is not the content of our heads but the greater being in which we participate.

When you die you drop your body. You drop all the memories and associations you've spent your life accumulating. These accumulations weren't you anyway. Why would you want to take them with you? The idea is to die to the self—to the ego—in order to wake up to being God.

Who knows what happens when we wake up from the dream of life? How will we exist? What we do know is that the promise of life after death keeps too many people from experiencing life in the present moment—right now—when they really do exist.

Afterlife is a nice notion, but it's a metaphor. It's a metaphor about hope and promise, and also a metaphor about undying love and nostalgia. Attending AIDS memorials has taught us that our friends live on in our fond memories of them. Most importantly, afterlife is a clue to the possibility of finding heaven *now*. For the time to be in heaven is *now* while you're alive. If you achieve that experience in life, afterlife will take care of itself. If you fail to, how will your ego be any better at achieving it when you're dead?

The myths of afterlife—and the "supernatural" phenomena on which the myths are based, like the "tunnel of light" report-ed by people who have near-death experiences—suggest that people who die with a keen awareness of their dying experience their final moment blurring blissfully (or torturously) into eter-nity. If you die happy—resigned to the inevitable, grateful and satisfied with the life you've lived and the love you've both given and received—then that happiness stretches out, for you, into a tunnel of light, crowded with loved ones, without end. If you die unhappy—fighting, resisting, and wanting to keep living because you aren't satisfied—then that state of emotional "hell" may seem unending. Perhaps as we human beings die and the structures in our brain that measure and order the perception of time shut down, we literally experience ourselves timeless: We never experience an end.

Indeed, the dead do live on in eternity in the sense that, outside the perspective of time, the whole universe from Big Bang to final crunch or whimper exists simultaneously: Present time is just a position of perspective along the space-time continuum. Everybody's alive at once. From a higher per-spective—God's perspective—everything is happening *now*.

This is why it's important to learn to pay attention, to be here now. It could be good preparation for dying. This is what belief in afterlife is supposed to encourage.

Myths of reincarnation exemplify the karmic vibes. The metaphor that the soul moves from one life to another, accumulating karma, really means that our lives in the present are influenced by the lives of those who've lived before us. Your "past lives" are really the vibes from the lives of people before you with which you particularly resonate in this life. In fact, your past lives are all the lives that human beings have ever lived. Buddha taught the notion of *anatta,* or no-self: What passes from life to life isn't an immortal soul but rather the karmic patterns that each life generates.

What the myth is supposed to convey to you is that you're not just your ego. You're not a lone, isolated individual struggling and competing with other isolated individuals. The ego is the intersection of vibes from all the lives—past and present—going on around you: all passing phenomena, all just superficial details. The ego is but a point of view. The real *you* is the consciousness itself generated through all those other lives. That's why you can extricate yourself from the details. Myths of reincarnation reveal the complex mental and spiritual environment in which we experience consciousness from our own unique perspective.

The myths of eternity, heaven, and hell reveal the depths and intensities of consciousness available to us right now, from our personal perspective. Eternity is the substance of all transient phenomena; eternity is consciousness focused on "being here now." Heaven is a state of mind in that here and now: one happy to go with the flow of life, free of judgment and opinion, blissfully aware of the wonder of being conscious *right now.* Hell is also a state of mind, one of general resistance to life and to change, full of judgments and opinions, ever unsatisfyingly attached to personal ego, always chewing over the past and thinking about the future.

We create our own heavens and our own hells right now in this life through our attitude toward life, toward other people, and toward the collective reality of the planet. If we will joy for others, our world begins to accumulate joy and we get to experience the joy too. If we will joy only for ourselves and resent it in others, we diminish the amount of joy in our own world and create hell.

Judging other people "wrong" is what produces hell on earth. Hell is the sum of negative judgments that people make about other people's behaviors, especially other people's experience of joy and pleasure. Homosexuality is the classic example—which is why it is so important in the current transformation of religion. Out of ignorance, resentment, and disapproval, society puts out bad vibes about homosexual feelings. These cause *all* people to be confused and conflicted about sexual urges. And they cause young homosexuals, in particular, to feel guilt and self-loathing. These are the pains of hell.

Forgiving others and understanding their behavior from their perspective frees you from your ego. Praying for other people's joy, forgiving them their trespasses against you, and wanting happiness for them creates heaven around you.

Prayer

But God doesn't hear prayers—at least not the prayers of those confused young homosexuals who plead to be free from their aberrant sexuality. That's clear enough to those of us who once prayed such prayers ourselves.

Similarly, God doesn't answer prayers to make the stock market go up. God doesn't give you an A on a test because you prayed fervently enough. Of course, believing you have God's assistance in researching investments or taking a test *can* help your portfolio or your score because the belief creates a self-fulfilling prophecy. Prayer isn't about changing God; prayer is about changing you. Setting up positive self-fulfilling prophecies is how most all prayer works.

Prayer doesn't work because of God's meddling. Prayer works because human beings have the power to influence the outcome of events. These powers are mythologized as God listening to prayers.

The myth of the God who answers prayers is a clue to the power of mind. The issue of prayer—using the mind to shape the outcome of events in the future—is a clue to the complex reality of consciousness. Prayer and miraculous healing sometimes works; this has even been verified by experimental research. There is power in human intentions. To pray to Jesus or the saints is to recall their example and to reach into your being to find the power they represent. To pray to the Blessed Virgin Mary isn't to make the BVM happy: It's to activate the feminine aspect of your own creative power, to shape with maternal and womanly wisdom your hopes for the outcome of events. It's to change how *you* see the world and how you decide what you want to create and how you should shape your intentions.

God, after all, has no opinions. God simply experiences being. We are most like God when we let go of opinions and judgments—all those traits we think of as personal. When we're not trapped in the mind-stuff going on inside our heads, we have greatest access to the creative powers. The reason not to think of God as personal—neurotic, judgmental, preferential, fickle, manipulative, "King of the World"—is to stop thinking of ourselves as personal.

Gay people should find it natural to understand religion from a higher perspective, having grown up as outsiders. Shrewd and cagey observers, we are especially attuned to others' pretensions because we are so keenly attuned to our own. We can see that the metaphor of God as a male king was a useful gimmick to prop up straight male authority, a pretense to allay males' fears and inadequacies.

A New Myth

A new myth is developing in human consciousness: a new understanding of religion that recognizes the metaphorical nature of the stories that have come down to us. A myth is a constellation of ideas that respond to the mysteries about life and the world and, especially, explain the death that all human beings must face. The myths we believe in give us a sense of our place in the cosmos, inspire us with awe and wonder, and teach us to love life. Myths have to seem true; they have to prompt us to respond: "Of course—this is the way things really are."

Myths have four basic functions: to describe the universe by explaining where it came from (creation, myths of origin), to communicate moral norms (heaven/purgatory/hell, karma), to create a sense of society and community (church, sangha), and to inspire mystical, ecstatic experience (signs and miracles, heaven).

The myths that have guided human development have evolved along with us. In *The Hero With a Thousand Faces*, penned in 1948, long before the feminist critique of language enlightened how we speak of humanity in the collective, Campbell wrote:

> The descent of the Occidental sciences from the heavens to the earth (from 17th-century astronomy to 19th-century biology), and their concentration today, at last, on man himself (in 20th-century anthropology and psychology), mark the path of a prodigious transfer of the focal point of human wonder. Not the animal world, not the plant world, and not the miracle of the spheres, but man himself is now the crucial mystery.

What inspires us with wonder today is the self-awareness of the consciousness that could have imagined God and the gods and that can now examine with telescopes and microscopes the complex, multidimensional cosmos. What inspires us is consciousness itself, seeing how it reveals itself to itself.

We could call this the "myth" of myth. It is awareness of the nature of the mythologizing faculty in consciousness that inspires meaning and wonder. From this perspective, the truth of the sacred stories lies in their meaning, not in the historical details that gave rise to them.

This way of thinking about religion is very different from the traditional way. It implies that the Resurrection of Christ is more about the survival of goodness and wisdom over tyranny and cruelty than about the resuscitation of Jesus in the tomb. It also means that the perpetual virginity of the Blessed Mother is more about the significance of her son's teachings than about the state of Mary's hymen, and that the creation of the world is more about the nature of consciousness than about planetary history or the origin of life.

On the one hand, this transformation looks to many like secularization and the breakdown of traditional belief, with all its messages about propriety, decency, and social order. Conservatives decry the ebb of religiousness, saying that something important is being lost. In some ways they are right. The purely scientific, materialistic, secular worldview can flatten reality, taking all the magic out of life along with all the meaning and value. Science only describes; it doesn't prescribe values or explain meaning.

On the other hand, this transformation looks, to others, like the discovery of the truths underlying the mythological traditions and an escape from all the superstitious, controlling, patriarchal accretions to the basic spiritual messages. They see these accretions have ruined religion. To them, finding the truth behind the metaphors is uncovering the experience of compassion that actually grounds the moral teachings. To these people—many gay men and lesbians among them—this transformation promises to save the best and most meaningful aspects of the religious traditions while getting rid of all the error, ignorance, and meanness.

Traditional religious ideas *also* flatten reality by shifting all the wonder, power, and magic into an external personal God totally separate from the physical universe. The aim of the modern transformation—signified linguistically by the trend in usage toward the term *spiritual*—is to rediscover the magic and wonder that founded religion in the first place. It's up to those of us awake to this transformation to explain spiritual meaning with metaphors that make sense according to contemporary worldviews and scientific models of reality.

The better metaphor of God is All That Is, the universal process of which we are all a part, not a self-aware outsider observer. *We* actually are the self-aware observers. We, human beings, are how God becomes conscious and personal.

Chapter 8
More Things Our Homosexuality
Tells Us About God

The new myth is evolutionary. A God that makes more sense for today is the God of universal process, the *élan vital* that moves through time, evolving greater consciousness. This is a God concerned with planetary ecology rather than individual cleanliness, ritual purity, or sexual behavior. This is the God hinted at in the Gaia Hypothesis—the idea that the Earth itself is a living being, a vast and complex entity composed of the interplay of all living creatures, all of which are organs of its planetary body. We human beings are the consciousness of Gaia, the brains and neurons of a global mind that transcends any sort of personality based on human perspective. Each of us is a sensory organ of Gaia, a window through which God takes in and experiences the world.

This God is not a personal being who plays favorites and who watches and judges human behavior. Rather, it is the planetary organism that grows, changes, and adapts to new conditions, gradually becoming more conscious and generating greater harmony and awareness. This God evolves out of and through human behavior and only watches and judges through us human beings. Pierre Teilhard de Chardin said human beings are evolution become conscious and responsible for itself.

Contrary to the fundamentalists' objections, the evolutionary model doesn't devalue human life. Indeed, it honors life by finding within life itself the purpose of being: endless profusion and ceaseless change.

Process-God

Modern "process theologies," like Teihard's, include evolutionary dynamics in the concept of God. The French Jesuit, for example, envisioned God as the goal of the evolution of the universe, the Omega Point. Once God has evolved through the universe, He in effect "pops out" of it and transcends time so that He then coexists with *all* time and can become the Creator of the Universe from the beginning. This process-God bootstraps himself into existence and the universe is the process by which this happens.

Such a process-God wouldn't hear prayers or meddle in human affairs. There'd be no reason to change anything. And changing things might screw up the outcome of the process. (This is the plot gimmick in sci-fi time travel stories called the "grandfather paradox.") But the vision of God as evolutionary process, rather than as an external, personal Supreme Being, does have practical implications for moral issues from abortion to overpopulation. It can help us see how *we'd* change things.

According to the aphorism "Ontogeny replicates phylogeny," during gestation each individual goes through *all* the stages of evolution of *all* life. Though microbiology and DNA research now show this idea to be simplistic, the basic metaphor—propounded by 19th-century German biologist Ernst Haeckel, who's also credited with coining the paradigm-changing term *ecology*—is still appealing.

During fetal development the growing human being replicates the whole course of evolution, going from one-cell to multicell organism, to fish, animal, and to human. There is, in fact, a period when the fetus develops gills; then as the specialization of organs continues toward full humanity, these structures become the eustachian tubes in the ears.

If the individual replicates the class, then the life of every human being replicates the evolution of God from hydrogen atom to complex universe to conscious being. Isn't this what it means to say: "Man is made in the image and likeness of God"? This is a beautiful idea. It places each of us in the long line of time unfolding and generating the complex cosmos.

In this evolutionary model, humanity evolves up through the nonhuman; there is a time when a fetus is not yet human. This differs significantly from conventional religious models in which God the Father infuses the soul at the moment of conception; in this model humanity is not a developmental process. There are great implications for the debates about abortion and embryonic cell research in which model you choose. According to the evolutionary model, abortions, IUD–based and "day-after" contraception, reductions in multiple embryos, or destruction of in vitro fertilizations could all be performed before human identity has evolved.

The model we choose ought to reflect contemporary worldview. If most people feel abortion is justified in certain situations, shouldn't their metaphor for life reflect a universe in which embryos can be terminated before they go through the multiple stages of evolution to become human? The religious model ought to change and evolve to keep up with the scientific model. Why would we want a religious model of the universe that claims its authority from the very fact that it is inconsistent with the modern worldview?

We're Part of the Earth

Throughout most of history the issue has been the survival and propagation of the human race as the carrier of consciousness. Religious myth was about maintaining the food supply and keeping the production of offspring ahead of the mortality rate. There had to be people to work the fields and soldiers to protect against the theft of resources.

Myth motivated people to endure in spite of threat, disease, or war. There were gods and goddesses of grain, farmer saints, gods of war, and militant angels like Michael the Archangel. Religious rituals and the liturgical cycle mirrored the progress of the year, celebrated the eternal return of the seasons, and kept society going and growing.

Today, the situation is different. Most of us live in cities. While we enjoy the passing of the seasons, now they're less about God and more about vacation spots and economic cycles. Now the problem is not in having *enough* people but in dealing with the fact that there are *too many* people. Those people are using up natural resources, polluting the air and water, and most importantly, producing more waste than the environment can reabsorb. Now it's the size of the human population—not wild animals, plagues, or enemy soldiers—that threatens the survival of consciousness on Earth.

One of the major effects of overpopulation—though not usually attributed to this cause at all—is the increase in scale of natural disasters. Many of these disasters are linked to global warming and the increase in energy in storm systems round the world. Global warming is itself a consequence of overpopulation: There are so many cars, so many power plants, and so many factories producing greenhouse gases because there are so many people.

But also the scale of disasters has increased because there are more people to be victims. The tornadoes that used to roil across prairie and wilderness now hit populated areas because there are simply more people inhabiting the land. Slightly heavier-than-usual rains now create floods and inundate homes because the trees and vegetation that used to slow the rush of the water have been cut down and people now live on hillsides and flood plains. Because cities have grown and pushed outward, people also now live in flammable forests and on the slopes of volcanoes. And in the cities, buildings have gotten taller so they can hold more people, and are therefore more susceptible to earthquakes—or terrorist attack.

God Would Be Concerned About the Survival of Earth

Most human beings don't seem to see that we're part of the Earth. Global warming, the disappearance of animal species, and the death of coral reefs tell us something is wrong with our current cultural mythologies. Even as their planetary home shrivels and dies, American Christians seem more concerned with preventing homosexuals from marrying or serving in the military than with saving the environment. Indeed, environmentalists are dismissed as "tree huggers" and equated with "liberals" and "Communists." There is no stronger evidence the mainstream mythology isn't working.

Theistic myths like Christianity and Islam envision God outside the planetary process. They describe afterlives in a nonmaterial heaven somewhere other than Earth. Their adherents presume God will save us (or at least them) from the devastation the human race inflicts on the Earth. These traditional religions concern themselves with minutiae while ignoring or denying the big issues.

In the first part of the 20th century—the time conservatives recall as the "good old days" in America—the world population was about 2 billion. By the beginning of the 21st century, the world population is up to 6 billion. While there are many other factors beside population that have changed since the good old days, most of those relate to the population issues. In order to return to the good old days, two out of every three people would have to be eliminated. The conservatives never mention that.

According to environmental experts, Americans use 30 times the natural resources per person as the rest of the world. Obviously, we could use a lot less—and probably be happier—but there is much that is good in our lives. Some of the affectations of modern life ought to be done away with, but many ought to be saved—and *made available to everyone on Earth*. If we like our lifestyle, then we ought to offer it to everybody, not just keep it for ourselves at the expense of everybody else.

To extend the modern American way of life to the entire world *and* to maintain the level of resources used worldwide at today's rates (which are already too high), the global population would have to be reduced by 30 times—29 out of every 30 people would have to go. Short of a devastating catastrophe, it's hard to see how that could come about. And such a catastrophe would set human development back centuries and wouldn't accomplish either bringing back the good old days or extending the good life to the world.

The Gay Solution to World Ecology

One way to reduce population is to increase the number of homosexuals and to popularize the idea that most people shouldn't reproduce. A familiar argument against homosexuality is the notion that if homosexuality is allowed, everybody will become homosexual and the human race will die out. Taking a reality check, we see that if everybody remains flagrantly heterosexual and reproduces heedlessly (which is what forces like the Catholic Church favor), the human race *will* die out, killed off by the irreparable damage to the environment.

It's baffling why opponents of homosexuality think recognizing homosexuality as natural will result in everybody's becoming gay. Is their heterosexuality so tenuous that they'd switch to our side if there weren't rules against it? And do they think homosexuals so shortsighted that, if indeed everybody on Earth decided to join us, an all-gay population of the future wouldn't figure out how to reproduce itself at sustainable levels? Clearly an all-gay planet—outlandish as that idea might be—could and would provide for the perpetuation of the species. The contrary argument simply demonstrates that straight people think gay life is only about homosexual sex— and that on some level they envy us and vigorously have to fight that urge to join up!

The model family touted by conservative Christians is generally the old-fashioned extended family with many children and many relatives all living in close proximity. This is not the hothouse nuclear family of two parents and two or three children living a tightly knit life apart from other relatives. Perhaps they're right that large families are best for raising children; such arrangements allow the children more independence and provide them with more role models. But if the goal is large families, in an overcrowded world we surely need fewer of them. Trained and licensed "professional" parents could raise families of six to 10 children with financial assistance from society. Then most people would need to live childless lives, focusing on improving the world for *all* of the society's offspring. Gay people would have a natural place in such a society.

It is very hard to know how many homosexuals there are. Surveys don't produce accurate data. Government censuses don't even dare ask the question, and the data would be unreliable anyway. It is even more difficult to know how many homosexuals there were at any given time in the past. Heterosexual domination and the persecution of homosexuals through the ages have effectively (perhaps intentionally) made it impossible to know. Some theoreticians hypothesize that the homosexual percentage of human populations remains relatively constant—usually the 10% figure popularized by the Kinsey research. But how can we know?

Obviously, though, there are more *gay* people now than ever before; that is, there are more people who are openly homosexual and who participate in gay-identified culture. That may or may not mean there are more homosexuals. But perhaps there really *are*. On a superficial level this is what everybody can see: 50 years ago nobody heard much about homosexuality; now it is everywhere.

There isn't a great deal else the collective planetary mind can do about population except give rise to human beings whose desires and predilections cause them to live in ways that don't result in progeny. Perhaps the appearance of modern homosexuality and gay identity is dramatic evidence that the Earth wants fewer people. At any rate, an increase in the number of gay people living full, contributing lives is a better solution to overpopulation than a devastating catastrophe.

It is telling that in the Bible story of Noah and the flood, Yahweh gives the rainbow as the sign He will never again bring about such a catastrophe. Now the rainbow flag has become the political and cultural symbol of gay community. Aren't we the manifestation today of that divine promise made in mythical time? There won't have to be a worldwide catastrophe, because we are the alternative solution.

Our homosexuality allows us to think these thoughts. They may be frivolous thoughts, but that's only because heterosexuals can't even begin to think them. They are so beyond the pale. The heterosexuals' God gives the command to go forth and multiply. We can imagine that God might have other priorities.

We don't have to recruit. No need for those toaster oven prizes. Nature keeps producing new members for our tribe. Even if all of us were killed off in a terrible fit of homophobic rage, in the next generation there would be just as many homosexuals as there were before.

What we need to communicate to the world is not that people should be homosexual and cultivate the styles of gay culture (though that's not a bad suggestion) but that people should be responsive to their deepest psychological needs, to what brings them bliss.

We don't need to tell people to be gay. We need to help

them speak the truth to themselves. Hearing this truth allows them to respond to the subtle messages Gaia communicates. After all, it is precisely through sex that Gaia/God communicates. Through our physical bodies Gaia makes itself known. That is what Gaia is: the collective bodies of all living beings on Earth.

Gaia and Yahweh

Gaia *is* evolution. Evolution *is* the expansion of the universe through time and space. God is the clue to the direction of evolution and the wake-up call to consciousness. We envision God and long to be one with God because that is our destiny.

Gaia is a better myth than Yahweh, the God of the Bible and the Koran. Gaia doesn't require belief against evidence (which religion considers a virtue but which is really just hardheadedness and willful ignorance). By contrast, Gaia is an experience, an intuition—not a metaphysical proposition. There isn't a personal Gaia, and there doesn't need to be for the intuition to make sense and to be moving—it's a reflection of life itself. Gaia is an intuitive idea and automatically exists as a result of understanding the idea.

Yahweh, on the other hand, is not an idea but a person. He either exists or does not exist. The personal God is a proposition that is either true or false. (That's what that stern lady meant when she accused Joseph Campbell of being an atheist.) Evidence has to be presented to demonstrate that the theological claims are true in the way they claim to be. And the lack of evidence tends to demonstrate that such claims are not true. That's why so many people can dismiss them or believe in other personal gods with different personal characteristics.

Yahweh—or any other personal God—requires acceding to somebody else's authority or testimony. You can't intuit from your own observation that in the past Yahweh didn't want people to eat pork or lobster, or that He later changed His mind and forbade meat on Fridays instead. You can't intuitively discern why He used to object to farmers' planting different grains in the same field (since it has turned out to be good husbandry) or why He no longer has opinions about such things. You can't intuit that He'd have negative opinions about homosexuals: The objection to homosexuals being homosexual is not obvious—at least not to homosexuals.

You can't *see* a personal God in nature. If you ascribe personality to nature, you've got Gaia, not Yahweh.

Gaia is perceived by rising to a higher perspective and seeing how planet Earth works. The ecology of life *demonstrates* the reality behind the myth of Gaia.

The notion of Gaia is, of course, a metaphor. Based in the vocabulary of Greek myth, Gaia is a modern metaphor arising from awareness of the ecology of planet Earth. Ecological awareness emerges from the experience of rising above the immediate world and discerning larger patterns. Such awareness can discern consciousness as a collective experience. The myth of the personal God who relates to human beings on an individual basis encourages emphasis on ego. The image of Gaia encourages a sense of collective being, for individuals are simply passing phases in Gaia's consciousness. The personal God is outside us. The collective God is *within* us— which is to say, we are within it.

Meditation

The way to connect with the greater reality is through interior meditation. For meditation is about experiencing and understanding the God within.

Meditation practice, as taught by the religions of the East and the contemplative saints of the West, and popularized by the New Age as part of the transformation of religion, is a means of changing ourselves and expanding our consciousness.

Meditation goes to the heart of the matter. Perhaps religious traditions are needed to transmit meditation techniques—though the church buildings scattered across the landscape sometimes look like the source of more harm than good, and in most of those churches people aren't learning how to meditate. But meditation and religious practice are not mutually exclusive. By taking up these practices we follow in the footsteps—and resonate with the vibes—of generations of gay men and lesbians before us who entered contemplative and monastic life and learned to practice interior prayer.

There's a Zen notion that if you want to be enlightened and to succeed at life, you must be able to do at least one thing right. You can start with something simple, like sitting. If you can't manage to sit right, the Zen masters say, how can you expect to do anything else right?

It's not so simple, though, because simply sitting means *not doing anything else.* This means you are not thinking. 'Cause if you are thinking—or remembering, fretting, anticipating, or planning—then that's what you're doing, not sitting. So the physical discipline is really a metaphor for a mental discipline.

How to Meditate

To meditate, sit comfortably in an erect, stable posture; preferably, but not necessarily, with your legs folded under you in the lotus or half-lotus posture and buttocks raised slightly with a pillow so that your spine is straight and elongated. You can close your eyes (Hindu style) or keep them open in soft focus on a spot an arm's distance in front of you (Buddhist style). Keeping your eyes open deters falling asleep. Rest your hands on your knees or cup them in your lap. Place the tip of your tongue lightly against the back of your teeth. Breathe regularly. Attend to your breathing and to the stability of your body. And hold the pose for 20 minutes.

The amount of time you commit is up to you. Twenty minutes is about the time it takes for the brain to fatigue and shift brain wave states, something akin to getting your "second wind" in athletics. However long you do it, you should decide the length in advance and stick to it. Set a realistic length and don't quit before the time is up. What you're feeling and thinking should have nothing to do with how long you maintain the practice. The success of the practice comes from doing it, not from your assessment of how well you think you're doing. That is, it has nothing to do with your ego. You can't do it wrong. So long as you sit for the time you predetermine, you're doing it right. You shouldn't daydream, fret about work, or plan your day's schedule, but if you do, then notice that and go back to just sitting. (Actually, a lot of creative work and planning gets accomplished just in watching the stuff bubble up into awareness.) If you need to scratch an itch, blow your nose, take a drink of water, or shift because your legs have fallen asleep, do so. Then smoothly return to the pose. The effort to maintain your relaxed but erect posture and to stick to your time limit will keep reminding you you're meditating. And that's what meditation is.

While you're sitting, time passes, you breathe, and you're aware. Focusing on the breath is the simplest technique for calming what's called "the monkey mind"—the tendency of the human mind to keep thinking and jumping from subject to subject. As you focus on your breath or simply on the passage of time, you'll find that monkey mind fills your consciousness with ideas, thoughts, opinions, and considerations. Just let them go and return to your focus of attention. In fact, by observing these fluctuations in consciousness with equanimity and letting them go, you accomplish *the* major work of meditation practice.

Transcendental meditation, the movement that with the help of the Beatles popularized meditation in the 1960s, teaches the technique of mantra meditation: recollecting the sound of a word given you by your teacher. TM says that the thoughts, memories, and associations that arise during meditation represent unfinished karma and unresolved business. Letting them come into consciousness without reacting to them discharges the karmic or emotional bond. Noticing them and then returning attention to the mantra gradually washes them away in the sound of the mantra.

This image also captures the healing power of psychotherapy. In the psychoanalytic technique of free association, the patient on the couch brings emotionally charged or repressed material into consciousness and discharges it by talking about it in a state of induced relaxation to his or her disinterested, nonreactive, and nonjudgmental analyst.

Other techniques for dealing with the monkey mind include gazing at an image (an icon, holy object, or candle flame), chanting a sacred word or phrase, ritualistically relaxing the body, focusing awareness on the seven chakras (power centers in the mind/body), remembering a particularly joyful or meaningful experience, or simply reminding yourself to "be here now." The point of any of these exercises is remind yourself that you're sitting and not doing anything else but sitting. (Indianologist and gay mystic Andrew Harvey helpfully describes a wide range of meditation techniques in *The Direct Path: Creating a Journey to the Divine Through the World's Mystical Traditions*.)

Most of the time our awareness tends to stay focused outside us. We live in our eyes and see the contents of our consciousness displayed as the outside world. When we sit in meditation we turn off the usual demands of the senses and allow our consciousness to rise above the particulars that drive our lives. By turning inward we start to see subtle aspects of our lives and our selves that are lost in the bright light of the outside world. The stars are still above us during the day, but the brightness of the sun makes them invisible. We don't see who we really are because most of the time we're blinded by our minds churning away.

A simple technique to redirect this churning is to use, like a mantra, the question "Who am I?" Such questions naturally arise as you sit. When you wonder "Who is meditating?" or "Who watches the thoughts come and go?" you discover "you" are not who you thought you were.

In earlier sections on projection and the Shadow, we learned that the brain is always involved in a process of identifying, sorting, evaluating, and filing current sense experience by associating it with events in the past and anticipating events in the future. This processing is the content of our lives. It is the activity of our egos. Your perspective on experience determines how you think of yourself. It's what "you" are. But there's another you that observes the processing. Because the ego is usually obsessed with the process rather than with present experience, you often don't even know who *you* are.

When it's not processed, experience is free of problems, suffering, fear, and desire. It's just what is, here and now. Meditation is training in the letting go of the obsession with the processing, thus letting go of past and future. Meditation teaches you to be aware of the present moment without the intervention of the mind by attending to the silence between thoughts. The silence *is* the moment of now.

A simple way to notice that silence and to drop the processing is to ask yourself: "What is my next thought going to be?" The "you" that awaits the answer is not your mind. Your mind is the processing function that produces the thought. But it's not the watcher.

To extend this exercise one step further, ask yourself: "What totally *new* thought am I going to have?" As the next thought comes up, observe it and see whether it flowed from what you'd been thinking previously. If it does, drop it—it isn't a new thought. Then wait for the next. When a truly new thought comes up, notice it and let it go, and watch to see whether the next thought is related to it. This practice keeps you mindful of the great silence from which thoughts emerge without letting you cling to any particular thought.

The "usual you" is the thoughts. Consciousness forgets itself every time it gets caught up in the flow of thoughts, ideas, experiences, and desires that you think of as yourself. When you allow thoughts to come and go, you can become aware of the space between the thoughts—the silence, consciousness itself. This emptiness between thoughts *is* the emptiness of space and the field of infinite potentiality. Being aware of the emptiness is being one with God. It is God—the One Mind—that is conscious in you.

Through meditation you begin to experience yourself as something deeper than the aggregate of your day-to-day sensory experience. You begin to discover the difference between experiencer and experience, between the dreamer and the dream, or—in W.B. Yeats's famous expression— between the dancer and the dance. Or, conversely, you discover there is no difference: There is no experiencer, only experience; no dreamer, only dream; no dancer, only dance. That is, there is no "you" separate from your experience, separate from the universe, or separate from God. The you that *seems* separate—your ego—is just the processing in your mind. It's not you. You are the universe—God—looking at yourself from the perspective of your history and placement in time and space.

The Physical Body, Vital Body, and Mental Body

Another set of meditation techniques involves becoming mindful of the space of your body and of the various layers or "bodies" that surround and comprise your consciousness. Buddhist psychology calls these "sheathes."

In meditation, when you deliberately narrow your focus and concentrate on simply sitting and breathing, you can feel the different layers of your own being. Most fundamental, of course, is your physical body, made up of matter that is, in turn, composed of biochemicals, molecules, and elemental particles. Atomic physics has discovered that these elemental particles are in fact mostly empty space—not things at all but energy fields that whirl across the surface of multidimensional space-time. From the perspective of the atoms that constitute our physical bodies, we are vast beings, larger than galaxies.

The physical body is inert matter, like a rock or a pile of soil. One day this body will die and return to dust. Even so, right now, it is *your* body, and it is clearly something more than material elements. It's alive. A complex array of biochemical reactions enlivens the physical body, including the digestion of food into fuel and the processing of that fuel with oxygen into energy. The aggregate of these processes is called the breath body. It's what you focus on in meditation practice; it's the "being alive" itself.

The breath body is porous and interconnected with other beings. In every breath you inhale particles that have been part of other beings' bodies and respirations. In every inhalation there are molecules that have been breathed by all the people who've ever lived. Indeed, in every breath you take are oxygen atoms that Jesus exhaled preaching the Beatitudes and Hitler rallying his troops to war. Because we are living beings, we are constantly exchanging the matter we are made of.

The exchange of biochemicals within this living matter directs the flow of vital energy. This is the hormonal body. It is also affected by biochemicals from the outside environment, like pheromones—the biochemical emissions from other people that are inhaled by the breath body. Your nervous system organizes and orients the activity of the body. The sensations and brain activity that ride on the life energy of the body constitute the neuronal body. This is what makes you sentient, aware of what's going on.

The breath body, hormonal/pheromonal body, and neuronal bodies are referred to collectively as the vital body. The vital body enlivens the physical body and gives rise to mind and spirit. The mental body is your awareness, the "stuff" going on inside your head. Not only are you receiving sensory input from your neurons, you are also making sense of it, cognizing it. Spirit, or soul, is the part of you that responds to experience and makes decisions, assessments, and judgments. In human beings, sentience, mentation, cognition, and understanding produce yet another layer of experience: meaning.

In this context, religion refers to the activities of the physical, vital, and mental bodies; sacraments, rituals, and beliefs operate on these levels. One step up, spirituality refers to the meaning behind the sacraments, rituals, and beliefs. Thus spirituality refers to the process by which human beings understand individual experience and the relationship between individuals and the cosmos. Spirituality refers to the operation of the radiant body.

The Radiant Body

Not only are you aware, you are aware that you're aware. You can observe yourself. This is consciousness, the part of you that grasps your understanding. It's the observer that registers sensations and assembles a universe of meaning. It's what "you" are. But it's also more than just you. This observing consciousness is the true mystery that inspires spirituality today. This is what our myths of God are about. This is what the practice of meditation is about. This is the meaning of those curious oriental statues of gods with multiple heads, one upon another: consciousness observing consciousness observing consciousness. By stilling sensory and mental activity, consciousness becomes aware of itself.

There is yet another layer or body that surrounds us. This is the part of us that gives off vibes. Modern radio and TV devices that resonate with invisible waves in the electromagnetic spectrum offer a metaphor for the "waves" or "vibes" that are radiated by sentience and vitality. Just as the flow of electricity through a microphone can be modulated to produce waves that can be transmitted to a radio receiver, so can the flow of electric charge and neurotransmitters in our bodies generate waves that other people can pick up. We generate them and we receive them. We receive them from the people around us and from the countless people who've lived before us. We may even pick them up from people who'll live after us; these vibrations may transcend time as we know it. Metaphorizing them as waves offers a scientific way of modeling such phenomena as telepathy, clairvoyance, prophecy, and past lives.

This sounds a little magical (and, in a way, it is). It's also very basic and very familiar: Happy people make the people around them happy. And the reverse is also true: Angry and unhappy people make the people around them angry and unhappy.

This outermost layer is composed of mentation, awareness, understanding, and intention. It can also be called the light body or the radiant body.

Human beings are only just beginning to understand how these mechanisms operate. We are influenced by our own intentions and by the intentions of all people as they interact with our interior process of world creation. Our karma—the causes and effects that result in observable patterns in our lives—comprises the resonances we pick up from all the lives around us and ahead of us. It is at this level that all the self-fulfilling prophecies and intentions, conscious and unconscious, of all people actually bring the world of experience into existence.

Sex as Meditation

Meditation allows us to perceive experience in a larger context by freeing us from the particulars. Sacred masturbation and tantric intercourse are forms of meditation that employ the powers of sex to focus the mind and transcend the particulars.

There are important parallels between meditation and sex—and, of course, important differences. Not all sex should be meditative. Sex with another person, especially a new potential lover, is almost entirely about the particulars. It's all about the senses, the experience of infatuation, and romantic love. But sexual arousal, either alone or with a regular partner, can be much more interior-focused. It can be about achieving states of transcendent consciousness. The replaying of karmic events and important memories can act like the techniques for discharging unfinished business. In masturbation—or perhaps in anonymous play at a sex club—the question "Who am I?" sometimes naturally arises. Sexual arousal can be an invitation to be mindful of consciousness—and to offer the greater consciousness pleasure and joy in creation.

Mirror-Gazing

Gazing into a mirror—especially deeply into one's own eyes—is a common meditation practice around the world. It dramatizes that question "Who am I?" by placing the questioner right in front of the embodiment of the question. Because the physical body that's reflected in the mirror is sexual, there's a sexual dimension to the question. This practice transforms self-image and expands consciousness.

Observe your own body in a full-length mirror, determining what you like and don't like about your looks. Honor your own body with the steady, consuming gaze you'd bestow on the body of any other attractive man standing naked before you.

As you gaze at your body—perhaps bringing yourself to sexual arousal—understand that what you're seeing is what other people see (though you never see yourself the way others do). This is how other people form their ideas of who you are and what you're like. This is how they find you desirable. This is also how you manifest yourself to yourself. This is how the spark of consciousness that is you imagines, visualizes, and projects itself into three-dimensional reality.

Then let your perspective rise as you settle your gaze on your eyes. This reflection is the universe. Inside the body you observe—in its brain, behind its eyes—is the entirety of the world you experience. And you're outside observing it.

See that you're not your body. You're the observer who is aware of what's going on in that body and who thinks in terms of the experiences that body has had. But you're something more. Your ego and self-image—all that stuff you think is so important—is just a reflection in the mirror of a consciousness that far transcends who "you" think you are.

Tibetan Buddhists say the practice of mirror-gazing allows one to see one's past incarnations. As you look at yourself in the mirror and peer deep into your eyes, let other faces rise to awareness. Imagine that what you're visualizing is the karmic patterns that intersect to shape your particular perspective. "You" are all the people who lived before you and whose karmic resonances create the context of your life. All the other beings are putting out vibes, just as you're putting out vibes. That's what the universe is. Allow that exalted vision to reside in and warm your chest and belly. Allow yourself to be sexually aroused by your vision and to see how the vast interplay of vibes comes into being in you as your flesh. Raise your perspective above time and realize it's all happening simultaneously. Be aware of your radiant body. In your mind's eye, see the radiance surrounding you.

If you bring yourself to orgasm, allow yourself to see that it's "God" you experience as pleasure. Feel the orgasm in your radiant body and let your pleasure radiate good, loving vibes.

The Birth of God

A couple of decades ago, radical theologians revived and popularized Friedrich Nietzsche's intentionally provocative declaration "God is dead" as a way of arguing that human beings are maturing psychologically beyond literal belief in the old myths. Even then, the issue wasn't so much the death of God as the *birth* of God.

Beginning with the Big Bang, energy has flowed into being, forcing space to expand and creating the context in which the universe exists. Space, carrying activity across its surface, evolves from chaotic energy into hydrogen atoms, then helium atoms, then on up the ladder of being to stars and planets. From there, the process spawns living, reproducing molecules, then plants, sentient beings, intelligent life, consciousness, and finally God.

God is the perfection of love, harmony, and beauty—the fullness of being, consciousness, and bliss. As we saw Teilhard hypothesized, once God evolves, it—or, mythically, "He"—pops out of time, becomes eternal, and coexists with all the stages of the process by which it developed through the universe. If the universe successfully evolves into God, then the being that is conscious in each of us self-aware sentient beings *is* God. If this is the case, "He" sees that everything is perfect in its place in the vast evolutionary pattern. There was never any such thing as evil.

If God fails to evolve—perhaps because we human beings render the Earth lifeless—then God, or at least this planet's part of the cosmic process, cannot pop out of time and observe that everything is good. Then everything *isn't* good; the process doesn't work out. The suffering and tragedy that generations of human beings and our predecessors have endured will have been for nothing. "Evil" will have won.

We cannot tell where we are in the vast process. We

cannot tell whether the being observing the universe through us is God existing co-eternally with the universe or just our individual egos suffering on their way to eventual oblivion.

Faith that God exists is faith that the universe works as it should and that evolution creates God. We *must* have faith that it will work, because that faith creates the self-fulfilling prophecy that brings it about. To believe in God, then, is to believe that evil isn't real and that it will ultimately be redeemed. To believe in evil is to put out the vibes—to prophesy—that God will not succeed. To overcome the belief in evil, you have to overcome the polarities. You have to see beyond dualism.

Our outsider perspective and our ability to transcend polarities makes us part of the self-fulfilling prophecy that brings God to life. That faith allows us to abandon judgment and concern for laying blame and to see that everything is perfect.

When God pops out of time, "He" sees all time in a single eternal moment. Similarly, when we see our lives from the present moment, *we* pop out of time and discover that the events of our lives comprise a single eternal moment; we discern how it all fits together. There is nothing to regret, nothing to resent. Thus we can forgive the universe, forgive all the individual assaults against us, and forgive the past. We can let it all go.

We can even forgive those televangelists—even the ugly-acting minister from Kansas. For we can see that it's not that they're wicked but just that their vision of God is too small. And they play an important role. By demonstrating how polarization and wrong-making corrupt religion, they inadvertently assist in its maturation into higher spirituality.

By letting go of judgment and the belief in evil, we participate in God's creation of Himself. Indeed, our experience *within* time is precisely God's experience *outside* of time—everything is perfect because together we managed to create God out of the cosmos.

Great Just the Way It Is

Thomas Merton ended his book, *The Sign of Jonas,* with words that echo that idea put into the mouth of God: "What was vile has become precious. What is now precious was never vile. I have always known the vile as precious: for what is vile I know not at all.... I have forgiven the universe without end, because I have never known sin."

And wise old man Joseph Campbell used to say: "People ask me, 'What about all the evil and suffering in the world?' And I say, 'It's great just the way it is.' " He'd stutter a little on the "g" and then shake his head as if in bewilderment that anybody could imagine any other response. "What else can you say? This is the way it is."

The purpose of meditation is to quiet the mind so that you can step outside your life for a moment and see what's going on, let go of the past, and transform the way you think about yourself and the universe. So you can forgive the universe. So you can say: "It's great just the way it is." Transforming your thoughts and intentions transforms the universe.

Even so, when we experience God's satisfaction with creation, we also experience God's impatience. All of nature groans with anticipation and restlessness as we human beings struggle to grow up and realize that everything is perfect just the way it is. That realization would end all the competition, hostility, blaming, and warfare that spoil the innate perfection. Nature is understandably impatient for human beings— straight men—to just stop all the dualistic bullshit.

As homosexuals who've been victims of that bullshit, we intuitively feel that Divine Impatience. Indeed, our impatience with "man's inhumanity to man" drives the gay cultural and political movement. That Divine Impatience is a spiritual manifestation of the physical expansion of the cosmos and the evolution of consciousness. Our efforts to achieve liberation and change the status quo—and our impatience with the social and, especially, religious forces that resist these efforts—is our participation in the creation of God.

This is a vision beyond duality and polarization. Though it points toward issues far beyond sexual liberation and the rebellion at the Stonewall Inn, we can see that, precisely because it calls for rising above duality, it's an insight that gay people can readily grasp and that we dramatize with our lives. That's why it's something our homosexuality tells us about the nature of God and the universe. And it's something that tells us how to transform our lives. In religious mythological terms, this is called "saving the world."

Chapter 9
Things Our Homosexuality Tells Us About the World

"The world and time are the dance of the Lord in empti-ness," wrote Merton in the conclusion to his mystical classic *New Seeds of Contemplation*. "[And] we are invited to forget ourselves on purpose, cast our awful solemnity to the winds, and join in the general dance."

Heterosexuality influences how human beings conceive the world and time. Built into everyday vision are notions of polarity and adversariness. This dualism appears in the models of the physical sciences. Physicists hypothesize that the universe is structured by competing forces; the primary forces are polarized into negative and positive; opposite poles attract and like poles repel. Isn't this just heterosexu-ality projected outward?

The heterosexual imperative "go forth and multiply" sug-gests that ever-increasing expansion and growth are good things. Our economic models prize expanding markets and increasing gross national product. Modern astronomy imag-ines the universe in a process of ceaseless expansion. Isn't this just more heterosexuality?

Because we gay people are creative, we think original and daring thoughts. We can conceive of the world and time in new ways. But everybody can do this. Imagination and cre-ativity are not unique to us. Still—and sadly—most people don't utilize them. The model of religion that honors faith and obedience to authority discourages and sometimes pun-ishes people for trying to think about the universe and God in new ways. Straight people—who already know their place in the cosmos—are not necessarily so motivated. Gay people, on the other hand, *are* motivated to find new explanations and new ways of conceptualizing our place in the universe in order to create that place.

Making Connections

All human beings need to connect. It's how we join in the general dance. Connection is what supports consciousness and human intelligence. People who can't form interpersonal connections are generally considered insane (infantile autism is the epitome). And sex is one of the major ways humans connect. How we think about making connections influences our experiences of life and love.

Built into the dualistic vision of the world is the notion that virtually everything links by heterosexual connection— opposites attract. Electrical connections plug "male" plugs into "female" sockets. Pipes have male and female joints and connectors. According to this mechanical model, homosexuality doesn't work because the "plumbing" doesn't fit.

There used to be a "homosexuality cure" called Aesthetic Realism. It argued that it is aesthetically pleasing that male and female fit together. By contrast, male and male and female and female don't possess the proper connectors and so are "unaesthetic." Of course, this ignored the fact that homosexuals find members of their own sex attractive. To homosexuals, homosexuality *is* aesthetically pleasing. Like most cures, Aesthetic Realism assumed homosexuality doesn't really exist.

Still, we don't have a model to demonstrate how male and male and female and female do fit together. We need an example of how, at the mechanical level, like connects to like. A model of homosexuality also needs to incorporate the "twist" that captures our reversal of the expected pattern. It is, after all, the "twist"—the fact that you have to discover something new about yourself, "come out," and transform how you see the world—that dominates gay experience. Our homosexuality is a 180-degree shift from what we would have expected.

The Queer Twist in Nature

The wedding band is a familiar symbol for the link between two people in sexual, spiritual, and karmic relationship. The band represents how two people become one, closing the circle, as it were. Though the body of the ring separates them, the inside and the outside of the ring come together in the unity of the closed band. Beginning with the image of the circle or band, let's introduce a twist with interesting properties that parallel aspects of gay consciousness.

In the topographical figure called a Möbius strip we find an icon for things connecting "homosexually." And it even does something "queer."

This figure is formed by taking a thin strip of paper (like adding-machine tape) and gluing the ends together to form a circular band. Sounds simple enough—but there's a twist: Left and right and inside and outside are switched. This creates a most peculiar construction. Forming the circular band transforms it from a rectangle to a cylinder, from two dimensions to three. But turning it back on itself *with the twist* moves that simple object into another kind of dimensionality altogether; it has a kind of queer infinity. It even looks like the infinity symbol. The surface area of the strip now contains both sides on the *same* side. The opposite poles have become each other. A Möbius strip is an unbounded surface with only one side and one edge: no inside, no outside, and no duality.

This is just a model, of course—an affectation. It doesn't prove anything. But like all mythological metaphors, it offers a way of thinking about and giving meaning to experience. It's a metaphor for the queer twist our gay identity gives to the world. It provides a rich, multilayered focus for meditation. Interestingly, this twisted figure eight pattern is the figure your folded legs form in the half-lotus meditation posture. When you sit in meditation, you're sitting in a Möbius twist—with your sexual center at the place of the twist.

We discover in the metaphor that this twist is just as much a part of reality as the male-female connections of plumbing but—in typically gay fashion—much more subtle in its implications. Homosexual personality blends masculine and feminine, bringing the polarities together and transcending them, putting both sides of human consciousness on the same side. The Möbius flip is connection by reflection, like the flip in a mirror image. Our beloved reflects our own gender, not a complementary opposite. Gay consciousness, like the Möbius twist, connects by reflection.

One of the most famous "twists" in the discoveries of modern science is the DNA molecule. The double helix of DNA replicates itself by untwisting and separating its two strands, then each strand links with free available amino acids to form an exact duplicate of itself, creating a new double helix. While the linking between the bases along the helical strands—adenine, thymine, cytosine, and guanine (A, T, C, G)—*is* key-in-lock, forming AT, CG, TA or GC pairs, the overall resulting strands are exact duplicates of the original— mirror images. DNA strands are not complementary opposites; there isn't a male strand and a female strand or even a right strand and a left strand. The DNA molecule reproduces by reflection—by forming a mirror image of itself. DNA replicates "homosexually."

Procreation occurs through key-in-lock connections—connections of opposites. Connection of likes—by reflection—generates consciousness. As we saw earlier, in the brain the neurons generate a mirror reflection of what the senses apprehend outside the body. This inner world is what we are conscious of as outside. Consciousness itself *is* our looking back at our own awareness as in a mirror, seeing what's inside as though it were outside. Our minds generate a world inside us that's twisted 180 degrees like a mirror image. In a curiously coincidental way, this twist is actually manifested in our bodies in the flip in the connections between the spinal cord and the brain: The right side of the brain controls the left side of the body and vice versa. Our bodies are mirror images of our brains. For every person, this inversion of inside and outside, left and right generates the "queer" dimension that *is* consciousness.

This consciousness is the consciousness of the Earth. Joseph Campbell said the most potent mythological image for our day is that of Earthrise from the surface of the moon. Human beings' going to the moon demonstrated, practically, the conquest of science and technology and, symbolically, the stance of consciousness able to be aware of itself. With the landing on the moon, for the first time, Earth was able to look back on itself from outside. This is how we now have to understand consciousness, not just from within but from without—by stepping outside, turning back, and looking at ourselves with an outsider's perspective. For Campbell, this symbolized the new myth: the "myth" of myth, spiritual consciousness understanding the nature of myth from over and above any particular mythological system—from outside.

All people are called to this perspective. Gay people are seasoned by our lives to assume it naturally. For to be gay is to have achieved such consciousness about oneself. A person can behave homosexually without being conscious of himself as homosexual, but to be conscious and to identify as gay is necessarily to have stepped outside and observed oneself and, therefore, to have understood one's life in a larger context.

Mystical Paradox

In the Gnostic Gospel of Thomas, Jesus offered a remarkably Möbius-like observation about the Kingdom of Heaven: "When you make the male as the female, and the female as the male, and the up as the down and the inner as the outer, then shall you see the Kingdom of Heaven."

Jesus *was* talking about twisting perceptions. This paradoxical thinking even appears in the canonical gospels: "The first shall be last and the last shall be first" and "To gain your life you must lose it." To see the Kingdom of Heaven, you have to change your perceptions; you have to look at the world a different way. Overcoming the polarities, seeing beyond male and female, is realizing such a transformation.

Around the same time that Jesus was preaching in Israel, a Buddhist tradition was developing in India that expresses a similar idea. Buddhist teachers, who wanted to dramatize the importance of compassion (seeing your *self* in others) as a religious experience, told the story of Avalokiteshvara, the attractive, lovable, and androgynous young seeker. Like Jesus, Avalokiteshvara saved the world.

This mythological character—called a Bodhisattva, one whose very being is enlightenment—is usually shown as a handsome young man sitting bare-chested in a relaxed meditation pose with one leg cocked or hanging casually over a wall. The story goes that he was just about to enter nirvana and escape altogether the cycles of rebirth that Buddhism understands as the true cause of suffering. But in that final moment he became so filled with compassion for the suffering beings he was about to leave behind that he volunteered to forgo nirvana to help others. In an act of world-saving generosity, he vowed to remain in the cycles of rebirth until all other beings had entered nirvana, and to take on himself the karmic debts of all those suffering sentient beings. At that instant, all sentient beings were saved and ushered into nirvana in distant mythic sacred time, leaving Avalokiteshvara alone behind to live out all their lifetimes and all their karma for them.

Avalokiteshvara is therefore the only Being that exists. He saves the world by becoming the world and all sentient beings—that is, all possible perspectives on the world. He saves the world by loving the world unconditionally, twisting the perception that the world is separate from him and that nirvana is somewhere other than here and now. He saves all beings—and himself—by shattering the distinction between nirvana and the world. The Bodhisattva lives in the "Kingdom of Heaven" because he inhabits the infinite Now.

Even as *we* experience the suffering of life in the world, we are all incarnations of the Bodhisattva. We are all that One Being. We have only to awaken to our true nature. And we do this by joyfully participating in the world out of unconditional compassion, by saying yes to life because that is what we have already done in sacred time as the Bodhisattva Avalokiteshvara.

This Buddhist myth reminds us of the links between our androgynous gayness, our delight in incarnation, and our search for spiritual insight. For there are Three Wonders of the Bodhisattva: The first wonder is that he transcends sexual duality, being simultaneously male and female. The second, that he transcends the difference between time and eternity, seeing no difference between earth and heaven. And the third wonder is that the first two wonders are the same!

The Bodhisattva's third wonder is like the twist in the Möbius strip, doubling back on itself and giving a whole new "dimension" of meaning to what went before. Androgyny *is* nirvana.

The metaphor of the "queer twist" in nature nicely captures the role gay people have played in society as promoters of culture and higher consciousness. We are the artists, poets, storytellers, designers, and creators of beauty who contribute not at the level of biology but at the level of mind. In meditation you feel the twisted figure eight in your legs. Furthermore, you can visualize the DNA in your cells twisting and untwisting, imagine your nervous system creating your internal world, sense your body as the mirror image of your brain, and conceive of yourself as planet Earth and look back at yourself from outside. You can remember being Avalokiteshvara. You can find a place for your own kind of consciousness, with your special kind of twist, in the basic nature of things.

You can even go one step further and perform the twist in judgment that repudiates all those male domination imperatives. Imagine yourself judging the world—like Jesus in Michelangelo's fresco of the Last Judgment in the Sistine Chapel. Observe all the sin and injustice in the world, all "man's inhumanity to man," all the failure, cruelty, and stupidity. And then twist the judgment and forgive it all. Will that all beings be welcomed into heaven and that none be cast into hell. Then you too are participating in saving the world.

Enlightenment Body

There is yet another "body" beyond the physical body, the vital body, and the radiant body. Understanding this is one of the developmental stages of the consciousness process called *enlightenment,* which is achieving the highest possible perspective on experience. It's both obvious *and* incomprehensible. This body—your true body, what you really are—is what you currently think of as the outside world.

Most of us, most of the time, think of ourselves as being *inside* our bodies, even up inside the geographical space of our heads. In fact, you are the fullness of your experience; you are your *whole* world. Though you're looking at things from a very specific and limited perspective—within the confines of your ego—your true body, the sheath that surrounds your consciousness and fills it with experience, is the cosmos. When you get this, you begin to understand that you are God, that there's *only* God, and that your finite existence is just a single point of view in a universe of infinite awareness.

Look around you. Don't you see you're different from other beings? Everybody around you has a head on top of his or her shoulders. But from your perspective, you alone have on top of your shoulders not a head but a world! Your consciousness isn't inside your head. It's manifest as the world. Our everyday conception of ourselves has it exactly backward. Everything in our experience is produced by the modulation of activity within the biological mass of our nervous/vital systems and is projected outward and perceived as the world around us. There's no real boundary between us and the world of our experience.

The way God knows you is not from outside, the way a person would. The way God knows you is from inside, by experiencing and regarding your experiences as you do. The self in you isn't a separate soul or a reincarnating ghost who inhabits your body while it undergoes some sort of ordeal. The self in you is God itself. That's why our lives and decisions are so important. They create the future. That's what the myth of God the Creator means.

We see God by reflection. God, the deep Self of the universe, manifests itself *to* us as our present experience and *as* us as our own consciousness. Our investigation into consciousness creates God, and we are that creation.

God acts in the world *as* us. We transform the world by recognizing that we are God evolving in the world. We really *can* do "magic" because everything is us. We are thought-forms created along the interface where we relate to other people, receive the vibes others emit, and mutually generate the world of common experience. In quantum physics this is called "collapsing the Schrödinger wave function" by which consciousness plays its part in the evolution of the quantum foam into universal Overmind.

This is the world you get to save.

Why the World Needs Saving

The world needs saving in great part because 2,000 years of Western Christianity and Greek philosophizing continue to project heterosexual dualism into our experience of our selves and our world. Dominated by alpha male imperatives (patriarchy, competition, hierarchy, scarcity, polarity, and right and wrong), people grow up thinking that mind and body, spirit and matter are separate and at odds. The unifying vision bestowed on us by our homosexual stance enables us to see that the various levels of the body and the different ways of viewing the world are just a matter of perspective. Each of us really has only one body—the cosmic body. There is no conflict between spirit and matter, no meaningful distinction between natural and supernatural. The apparent split between body and soul is just an echo of the difference between female and male.

You save the world by loving your own little corner of it. The psychiatrists are right that believing you have to "save the world" means taking on too much. There's no way any one of us can eliminate all human suffering and bring peace and harmony to the world. Thinking your life is a failure because you can't effect cosmic change is a sign of megalomania. Alone, you can't do anything to change the whole world. But you can do quite a lot to change your *own* world. That's how—together—we all change the greater world.

You save your own world by letting go of the past, forgiving the injustices you have suffered, and acting to solve problems without blaming other people for them. In other words, you save your world by seeing love and good intentions around you and by giving everybody in your immediate environment the proverbial "benefit of the doubt" by not making them wrong. When you live this way you become Avalokiteshvara taking on your karma and your life.

An interesting implication of this mythological image is that the same being in you is in everyone else. That beautiful man you smiled at on the bus or in the bar *is* Avalokiteshvara and *is* you. There's no one who isn't you. The hot men fucking in the porn videos—they're all the Bodhisattva fucking himself with infinite tenderness, compassion, and love for himself, which is manifest in every person. The hot men whom you long for are indeed you looking at the experience of the world, just from a different perspective. There need be no pain in the longing. You can realize joy in the joy of others. The longing itself is the pang that accompanies your realization of your oneness.

Bliss Body

The cosmic body is also called the bliss body. For, from your outsider's perspective, you see that you are not who you thought you were. You are not your ego. You are not your mind—that little voice that chatters on incessantly inside your head. As we've seen, that voice—that ego—is the brain processing its data, associating new experience with old. But it's just the processing system. It's not you. You are the witness observer that is conscious of the process. The trick is not to get caught in the watching and forget you're the watcher. The watched process exists in the past and the future, in memory/judgment, and in expectation/preparation. The watcher inhabits the present.

When you bring your attention to the present, you see

that you are the Cosmic Self—pure potentiality and pure consciousness—choosing to incarnate as your particular perspective out of pure curiosity and love for existence. The bliss body is Being itself being I Am. This, after all, is the meaning of the name of God: I Am Who Am.

The outside world is "you" spread across the surface of your experience. Your ego, your life, is all that stuff you have opinions and make judgments about, all the stuff that fills your consciousness. Even the little voice in your head is just part of the stuff. Conventional thinking tells us we're inside our bodies and God is ultimately outside us. But it's really the other way around. What's outside—the stuff—is "you"; what's inside—what is having the experience—is "God."

There's a pun in the Sanskrit syllables that form the name Avalokiteshvara. Parsed one way, the syllables mean: "The Lord Who Looks Down in Pity." Parsed another, they mean: "The Lord Who Is Seen Within." Reflection causes you to look at your experience; consciousness turns back on itself. Make the Möbius flip and you ascend to mystical consciousness and sense your oneness with the cosmic Self, the bliss body. Then you see you are your world.

All people are called to this enlightenment to free themselves from suffering (the product of fear and desire that exist only in relation to the past and the future) and to take responsibility for the state of creation (out of compassion for all beings). Straight people are called to this consciousness through their experience of being responsible procreators. Gay people are called through our experience of being marginalized outsiders, sentinels on the far frontiers of consciousness.

The solution to suffering at the level of body and social interaction is Jesus' instruction: Love one another, be good to one another, don't make enemies, see yourselves in one another, be compassionate. And the solution to suffering at the level of mind and interior processing is Buddha's instruction: Be mindful, don't judge, see yourself as a momentary flicker of the flame of consciousness, and let go of all attachments.

The way to control the vibes you put out is to control the words you speak. This is why "right speech" is on the Buddha's list of instructions for following the path. After all, your words are the first level of your self-expression. What you say out loud is what other people hear and react to. It's how you influence the world outside you and how you create self-fulfilling prophecies. Most importantly, it's how you discover, yourself, what you really believe and intend. It's how you shape your own consciousness. Being mindful of the words you use allows you to shape your consciousness intentionally. If you use rude and angry words, you'll likely end up surrounded by rude and angry people and events. If you use gentle words, you won't reinforce hurt and anger or stress yourself out with ugly self-fulfilling prophecies, and you'll end up surrounded by gentleness.

You also control the vibes you put out by controlling the vibes you take in. The media will fill your mind with images of war and crime if you let them. In male-dominated society these images are presented as entertainment. But you don't have to accept this poisonous pabulum. You can opt for comedies instead of crime dramas, Broadway musicals instead of war movies. You can opt to think about love and sex instead of violence and mayhem.

What you think matters, because it affects the vibes you put out. Not only must you control your words; you must also control your mind. Unconscious, suppressed thoughts still have the power to determine behavior; witness the Freudian slip. That's why "right intention" is another of the Buddha's instructions for following the Eightfold Noble Path. You control your mind by becoming aware, being mindful, and intending to see peace and love rather than hostility and rancor.

We create—and save—the world by demonstrating a gay paradigm of creation just as real as the paradigm of key-in-lock procreation. Both are true, though the former is more mystical than the latter (because it deals with the nature of consciousness, not biology). Our lives demonstrate that people can—and should—have a good time. Joy and happiness are the purpose of life. What is within is a reflection of what is without. What is without is transformed by the perception of it by what is within. This twist demonstrates transformation. Therefore joy and happiness within generate joy and happiness without.

Joyful Participation in the Sorrows of the World

We can only really be happy and joyful when the people around us are happy and joyful. Therefore we want everyone to have the same good things we have. We save the world by revisioning the world. By changing our own consciousness we change how we see the world, and the world follows suit. We bring love and joy into the world by being loving and joyful and by acknowledging these qualities in others. We put out good intentions by rejoicing that we're alive and conscious, by loving unconditionally, by exercising compassion and generosity toward all sentient beings, and by living good, gay lives and putting out good, gay vibes.

Influential social activist and openly gay Episcopalian priest Malcolm Boyd says: "I really do believe that we as gay people have an involved role in the world. I see gays as a kind of perpetual Peace Corps. We are meant for something far beyond ourselves and our own selfish concerns. This is a part of the meaning of being gay."

The Buddhist spirituality mythologized in the story of Avalokiteshvara is called "joyful participation in the sorrows of the world." The Bodhisattva steadfastly regards human suffering and the struggle of life against life. He sees man's inhumanity to man. He observes injustice. Rather than retaliating, he forgives and embraces it all as nothing more than a passing manifestation, a downward eddy in an ascending current, a ripple in the peace of eternity. The Bodhisattva sees that suffering and evil are but the foreground of a wonder. He raises his eyes to the wonder and lets go of judgment and resistance. "It's great, just the way it is."

Miracles

This is the advice also of *A Course in Miracles*, the "revealed text" of a postmodern Christianity dictated to a Jewish psychology professor at Columbia University in the 1960s in the voice of Jesus himself. The Course in Miracles was embraced by many gay men in the early days of AIDS, when miracles seemed their only hope. However, the Jesus of the Course didn't promise outside interventions or suspensions of the laws of nature. The miracles of the Course are instances of life working smoothly because people help each other and hold good intentions for one another.

A Course in Miracles tells us we don't regularly and easily perform miracles because we fear we are in competition with God. We don't know what we should want for others and for ourselves because our minds are clouded by negative memories and associations from the past and by fear of God's retribution in the future. The dualistic, male-dominant worldview has such a hold on us that we mistrust our own good intentions and think we must surrender our power to a jealous God.

We don't have to surrender to that dictatorial and arbitrary God. Instead, we can participate joyfully and generously in an evolutionary God. Miracles are natural; life *should* work. The problems that are part of being human come and go, resolving themselves in the course of life itself. The only thing we need to change is our own attitude.

Sex Magick

Some gay spiritual groups are experimenting with the practice of sex magick. This is the ritualized use of sexual arousal to put out good vibes, not unlike church groups who pray for the welfare of the world. Sex magick is practiced through erotic massage, mindful masturbation, and tantric intercourse. Sex magick also involves "inner work" and group consciousness-raising, which bring into awareness, for discharge, the array of negative feelings that affect one's experience of sex. Men are urged to examine the roots of their feelings of attraction and repulsion toward other gay men to bring to light the shadowy roots of neurotic compulsions.

One reason the world is so screwed up is because the good intentions and karmic vibes have been distorted by the antisex attitudes that persist in most places where traditional religions continue to influence hearts and minds. To overcome the negative influence is the reason to practice sex magick. The goal is to put out good vibes.

Using the metaphor of the Mystical Body of Christ, Saint Paul (in 1 Corinthians 12) compares the different functions of people in the church to the different organs in the human body. All of us are organs in the Body of Christ. Following this metaphor, we might say gay men play the role of the penis of the Body of Christ (and lesbians, that of the clitoris of this sexually androgynous body). For we gay men understand—and witness—that the experience of sexual pleasure is healing and satisfying. The release of sex-related neurotransmitters and hormones keeps the body healthy and vital. Sex is good for people, and the cells in the penis put out good vibes for deep connections. In Body Electric training, penises are called by an honorable, if light-hearted, euphemism: wands. Wands work magic and miracles. It is good for the Mystical Body of Christ to have properly functioning erogenous cells. It is good for planet Earth that there are creative people who blend gender, have great taste, enjoy sex, and know how to use their wands.

When you're coming, think "Here comes God." And as you're writhing in the pleasure of orgasm, think "May all beings be happy. May all beings be free."

We Are All One

Spiritual work is overcoming ego. That's what the myths are all about, and that's what morality is about: overcoming the limitations of individual perspective so you can see beyond yourself. When personal issues no longer matter, the continual processing of time in the brain ceases to enthrall and you begin to live simply in the present. All your memories mean nothing. In gay-camp jargon this is put, "Get over yourself, Mary!"

The mystics say their goal is oneness with God. When you get over ego, you *are* one with God. That's what our new paradigm reveals. With that understanding you can appreciate the wonderful and various ways your life manifests cosmic truth. You can weave together the metaphors and symbols of art, religion, myth, literature, and culture. You can create meaning in your life, for this meaning is what the cosmic process has created you for.

Of course, there will be tragedy and occasional bad luck. Being a good person doesn't protect you from misfortune; the rain falls on the just and the unjust alike. But being "enlightened," having a good attitude, and accepting things as they come will make it easier to deal with tragedy. And putting out good vibes may, in fact, protect you from some tragedies.

Certainly your reaction to problems can worsen them. Getting hysterical and thrashing about won't solve anything and can create another level of difficulty. Taking things in stride and confronting problems with the kind of dispassionate interest one learns in meditation practice are likely to make difficulties easier to cope with. The various mythologies about karma, destiny, and poetic justice suggest that loving your experience more and resisting less will raise your vibration level and improve your "luck." If these notions work as self-fulfilling prophecy, then they turn out to be true.

Live as Though the Day Were Here

Nietzsche said, "Live as though the day were here." The way to save your own world—and the world at large—is to start living the way you want the world to become. There are no preliminary steps to be taken. We cannot wait for the rest of humankind to wake up; waiting only encourages them to sleep. As the mystics say: Now is the only time there is. Now is eternity. We can't wait for "the old farts" to become desensitized.

The same must be said about religion and religious belief. We see change happening. Every day another old superstition crumbles to dust. The human race is waking up to the greater mystery of the universe. There's no reason to wait and no reason to hold on to old-time religion. If we hope that in 20, 50, or 100 years people will think differently—less superstitiously—then now is the time to start realizing that vision.

In the long run, institutionalized religion as we've known it will be replaced by a scientifically sound and psychologically sophisticated view of life. This enlightened worldview will likely be based on Buddhistic moral and mystical perspectives, stripped of orientalisms and liberated from traditional antisex and antifemale biases, and enriched with the social teachings of Jesus, stripped of supernaturalism and freed from the institutional concerns of an organized church.

This transformation is happening in us and through us. Let us embrace and champion it. Let us reclaim our role as shamans and spiritual guides. Let us work to re-create religion so that it assists progress and doesn't impede it. Let us work to redefine and thereby re-create God so that the idea calls us into the future. Let us look to the future for truth, not to the past. The Golden Age, life in the Garden of Eden, is here with us now, not ahead of us, not behind.

Right now, as you're reading this book, the universe— that is, God—is manifesting itself to you *as* you. And this is the case throughout your life, whether you're attending to it or not. The image of God you hold in mind indicates how you think about life. In fact, you can change your life by changing how you imagine God. Tell the truth. Be who you are. Be loving and love life. Forgive. Be generous. After all, you're only giving to your true self. There is no reason to hide and no reason to be selfish or miserly.

All the stories of gods and heroes are not about supernatural beings and ancient events. They're about *you*, here and now.

This was Joseph Campbell's great message. The myths of religion are clues to each of us to what reality really is, and religion is a process in the eternal present, not the mythic past.

At the end of *The Hero With a Thousand Faces*, Campbell wrote: "The modern hero, the modern individual who dares to heed the call...cannot, indeed must not wait for his community to cast off its slough of pride, fear, rationalized avarice, and sanctified misunderstanding. It is not society that is to guide and save the creative hero, but precisely the reverse. And so every one of us shares the supreme ordeal—carries the cross of the redeemer—not in the bright moments of his tribe's great victories, but in the silences of his personal despair."

Jesus' saving acts didn't happen in Jerusalem two millennia ago; he didn't live, die, and rise again in historic time. Jesus' saving acts are happening right now through *you*. By loving your neighbor, seeing beyond religious and superstitious rules, and calling for goodness and loving kindness in your life right now—carrying your cross—you save your life and the lives of those around you.

Buddha's enlightenment wasn't about the great discoveries of a remarkable, saintly man who lived in Indian 500 years before Jesus. Buddha's enlightenment is about how *you* can wake up to the causes of suffering and the ephemeral nature of ego and human selfhood, right now. The story of the Buddha is really about you as you struggle to cope with the facts of sickness, old age, poverty, and religious renunciation. As you walk the Path you become a source of generous, self-less good intentions. All the stories of the gods are metaphors about how *you* can live a good human life.

Conclusion
Carrying the Cross

It is not a negative, fatalistic, or materialistic secularism our homosexuality reveals to us, but a universe full of mystery, wonder, beauty, and magic. But it's not the universe described by the authorities of religion. As old-time religion fades into the past along with other superstitions, a new vision of the universe emerges. And we're helping to bring this about.

We are all one. This is the central message of the new myth: one ecology, one planet, and one consciousness. This has been expressed mystically in the image of Christ's Mystical Body and Avalokiteshvara's vow to be all beings. It's now expressed in the image of Gaia, the planetary organism.

Archetypally, being homosexual means opting out of time. Choosing a life outside the cycle of birth, reproduction, parenting, and death—outside the round of natural being—is choosing to stop the cycle of time. Being gay witnesses to life lived in the present moment.

Of course, many homosexuals remain stuck in time—suffering the emotional and psychological damage of homophobia, reliving past hurts, and dreaming of future liberation. They do not live in the consciousness of the present. Nonetheless, the existence of homosexuality demonstrates life lived outside of time and beyond the polarities in the eternal moment of Now.

Our homosexuality urges us to develop a new paradigm of God and the universe because the old paradigm does not include or recognize us. At the same time, we must reclaim the wisdom of ancient, prehistoric eras when our spiritual and religious role in human culture *was* recognized and our two-spiritedness was a sign of the divine process at work in human society and consciousness.

Perhaps the gay role in the history of religion—after we have served as the liturgically creative and sexually confused priests and monks all these years—is now to tell the truth about the nature of religion and to celebrate sex and human incarnation openly. Perhaps we're here to proclaim a return of the true wisdom of Jesus, free of the superstitious and supernatural nonsense; that morality is based in compassion, not rules and taboos; that people should simply respect each other and behave with kindness and sensitivity. Isn't it the gay men in modern society—not the TV evangelists and right-wing commentators—who demonstrate true kindness and sensitivity?

We must find enlightenment within our homosexuality. We certainly can't find it without it. This is our spiritual path, the cross we must take up. All our lives we've been told our homosexuality will keep us off the spiritual path, that we must accept renunciation of sex as our cross. There's an irony here.

To make sense of that negative-sounding metaphor, we have to understand Jesus' passion and suffering, symbolically. The cross isn't about suffering; it's about transforming vision.

When Jesus was nailed to the cross, his arms and body were extended in the four directions of the compass. The cross represents incarnation in the material world. He was wounded in five places. The wounds represent the five sens-es. The crucifixion and resurrection indicates how the mate-rial, sensory, three-dimensional world is transformed by accepting incarnation—and death—without resistance. Jesus' cross was not just his suffering—it was also his redemption of the suffering by surrendering to it and seeing beyond it.

Your surrender allows you to participate in the salvation

of the world. This is the same as the Bodhisattva's vow to take on all incarnations and to accept life just the way it is. Surrendering to your homosexuality means accepting the role of outcast and prophet. Finding your own spirituality becomes your spiritual path.

Live, therefore, as though you were God taking on the karma of your life for you. Indeed, forgive all beings their karmic debts to you and choose to live the life you are living. Embrace the problems, frustrations, and joys that come with the body you live in; accept its attractiveness and its unattractiveness. Accept your life with its history and its level of accomplishment. Ebrace as well, of course, your level of dissatisfaction and political commitment and zeal to change things. Actually, you have no choice. All you can do is resist (by keeping your consciousness in past and future, in thoughts instead of experience). The only way to have your actual present experience is to choose it. This is what is symbolized by God's act of creation.

These words, which convey the necessary wisdom, appear on screen at the end of the Audrey Hepburn/Mel Ferrar film *War and Peace:*

> THE MOST DIFFICULT THING—
> BUT AN ESSENTIAL ONE—
> IS TO LOVE LIFE,
> TO LOVE IT EVEN WHILE ONE SUFFERS.
> BECAUSE LIFE IS ALL. LIFE IS GOD.
> AND TO LOVE LIFE MEANS TO LOVE GOD.
> —LEO TOLSTOY

We conclude with the most obvious—but most often ignored—message of all. Homosexuality tells us that life and God are much bigger than any of us can conceive, that nobody has a corner on the truth market, and that the only thing to do is to love one another. God is a clue to the deepest reality of consciousness. We experience God by experiencing life from our particular limited perspective. Though we're almost always blind to this fact, we see the face of God in our everyday experience. Everything that happens to us is God struggling for Self-knowledge through us. We human beings are the personal self of God.

Recognizing this allows us to say yes to life, to love life just as it is. When you love everything just the way it is, you see you are in heaven. And behold, it is very good! This is the saving message behind all religion and spirituality. This is what our homosexuality tells us about God and the universe.